Dog Adoption

A guide to choosing the perfect "preowned" dog from breeders, dog tracks, purebred rescue organizations & shelters

By: Joan Hustace Walker

ICS BOOKS, INC.
Merrillville, Indiana

Publisher's Dedication

This book is fondly dedicated to the memory of Jack,
a loving companion who was able to share his life with others,
and to Murphy, who was never given the chance.

Dog Adoption
Copyright © 1996 by Joan Hustace Walker
10 9 8 7 6 5 4 3 2 1

Published by:
ICS Books, Inc.
1370 E. 86th Place
Merrillville, IN 46410
800-541-7323

Library of Congress cataloging–in–Publication Data

Walker, Joan Hustace, 1972–
    Dog adoption: a guide to choosing the perfect "pre-owned" dog from breeders, dog racetracks, purebred rescue organizations, and shelters / by Joan Hustace Walker.
    p. cm.
    ISBN 1-57034-058-7 (pb)
    1. Dogs. 2. Dog breeds. 3. Dogs–Selection. I. Title.
SF426.W345 1997
636.7'0887'0297–DC21

96-51624
CIP

Table of Contents

Publisher's Foreword

Jack moved in with me when he was about 8 years old. I had known him, however, since he was a youngster as he was initially adopted by a mutual human friend. I could never bring myself to feeling that Jack was "owned." His personality was so advanced that, while he was not an equal, he was a certainly a full partner in life's adventures, taking the good moments along with the bad. Being an avid canoeist, Jack was able to repeatedly demonstrate his superior sense of smell and hearing while on wilderness trips. Well, I am not sure how avid a canoeist he was. He probably tolerated canoeing because he knew I liked to do it and he was interested in anything that I was doing. In the process he canoed twice into Hudson's Bay; he rafted the Rio Grande between Mexico and Texas; and he camped, hiked, and canoed numerous places in between. Jack was a master at sneaking into (and out of) hotels. While he may have personally considered it a game, he realized we regarded it a serious business.

Now I mention all of this not because I think people are interested in finding a dog to sneak into hotel rooms with them, nor do I necessarily advocate doing such a thing. But I wish to simply hint at how ingrained into one's life an animal companion can become. Jack was a full-fledged member of my extended family. And he was truly loved for what he was: a kind, compassionate and whose only purpose in life seemed to be to please us, to protect us and to eat, of course. And an occasional romance.

Of all of the numerous great moments which I shared with Jack, I realized that the most poignant was the moment of his death. Finally suffering from irreversible heart failure, he let us know it was time. Breathing became more labored, the coughing wouldn't respond to medication and then he stopped his beloved eating. When he refused my hand held offering of a small piece of home-cooked beef, I knew it was time for the last trip to the Vet. I am glad that I could be with this loyal friend during his last moment.

Although I am sure he knew it was the end, I tried to be up-beat and positive about becoming sleepy a word that he knew. While I am a physician and a Vietnam Veteran, I can tell you that it was the hardest thing I have had to go through in my life. Yet I am grateful for the chance to have been there for him.

It makes me pause to reflect on the incredible number of these intelligent beings who face death long before their allotted time. And who must face it under terrifying conditions. And alone. It has to still be dreadful to face death, even in the reassuring arms of your human friend. But what a horror to be stored with terrified others, to be shoved into a chamber and to have the air sucked out of your lungs, or to be injected with air, or potassium chloride, or sodium pentothal by an uncaring or at least an indifferent executioner while still at your prime while you are still filled with the God-given innate will to live and to thrive. Its an unimaginable fate except for those who have been subjected to a human holocaust.

We you are the only line of defense against this happening to a fellow, intelligent creature. By adopting the abandoned dog you have invited into your life not just a pet, but a potential fellow traveler through life. A provider of comfort, security, and love.

The purpose of this book is to dispel the resistance to adult dog adoption that some might feel. After all, what was wrong with the dog that somebody got rid of it? The truth of the matter is that the dog became inconvenient. While a dog shows tremendous loyalty, we humans generally do not. A divorce, a move into an apartment or across the country, acquiring an allergy, or the death of the owner are all reasons for the dog being dumped at the pond. While this is a virtual death sentence, I am sure that usually the humans go away hoping that someone will rescue it. That doesn't usually happen. There is no magical, mystical mob of people lined up to rescue these animals. The only hope is you. The death sentence stops here, with you. And, potentially, an important phase of your life also starts here. The phase that includes a new best friend.

William W. Forgey, M.D.
Editor, ICS Books.

Introduction

Every year, millions of adult dogs are euthanized in the United States. Unwanted mixed breeds, purebreds, and track dogs (Greyhounds) all meet the same fate if a good, second home can't be found for them. Fortunately, because of people like you who are interested in adopting or buying an adult dog and because of the tireless hours spent by rescue workers across the country, there are many adult dogs who do find homes.

Unfortunately, most unwanted dogs do not have a happy ending. Of the 3,000 shelters surveyed by the American Humane Association in 1992, 10.4 million dogs were either surrendered to shelters or picked up as strays. Of those dogs, 25% were placed with new families, 14% were reunited with their original owner, but 61% were euthanized. (Other sources report only a 10% adoption rate nationwide.)

According to a recent study conducted by Gary Patronek, Ph.D., graduate program coordinator at the Center for Animals and Public Policy, Tufts University, dog owners that did not participate in obedience classes with their dogs and those that did not seek proper veterinary care for their pets, were much more likely to relinquish their dogs to a shelter. "What this tells us is that people expected a certain type of behavior from their dog and that's not what they got," says Patronek. "It also suggests that the owners simply weren't prepared for the amount of work involved in dog ownership."

Patronek's study also indicates that adult dogs are much more likely to be surrendered to the shelter than puppies. And, according to shelter directors, adult dogs are much less likely to be placed than their youthful counterparts. It doesn't take a great amount of mathematical genius to figure out who is getting the short end of the stick.

Keep in mind, too, that death at a shelter is never pleasant. Elizabeth Vlk, senior humane educator with the National Humane Education Society, says that even though there are methods of euthanasia available to shelters that are relatively pain free, there are still shelters across the country that use other methods, ranging from taking the dog "out back" and shooting the animal in the head (sometimes not too accurately) to high-altitude chambers, electrocution, and injections of sodium chloride - all of which are acutely painful to the dog. "There are no laws that I know of that regulate how an animal is euthanized," says Vlk. "The method of euthanasia is pretty much set by the board of supervisors or board of directors and the organization's ability to find the funds. It boils down to what is the most cost-effective method."

As ugly as the picture is for the future of unwanted dogs, it shouldn't be the reason you choose to own a dog. I know this sounds contradictory, but dog ownership is not for everyone. In fact, that's part of the reason there are so many unwanted dogs in our country. Just as in the poem, "The Puppy in the Window," people often buy puppies and dogs on an emotional impulse without having any clue what kind of commitment and financial involvement is involved. Then when their bouncing bundle of fur becomes too inconvenient, the owners dispose of it. So, please be sure to examine your lifestyle, time constraints, financial concerns and level of commitment before you purchase a dog.

If, once you've carefully assessed your situation, you are ready, willing and able to make a lifelong commitment to a dog, I sincerely hope you will consider adopting an adult dog. There are many, many advantages to adopting or buying an adult dog. With few exceptions, you will receive back tenfold from your new life partner than what you put into the human-dog relationship.

If you choose not to adopt an adult dog, don't feel bad!!! If your lifestyle is currently not suitable for a dog, then don't torture yourself (and the dog!) by trying to make a difficult situation work. You should be commended for deciding to wait until your lifestyle changes to the point where you and a new dog would be very happy and comfortable.

But while you're waiting, why not consider supporting one of the many organizations that work toward placing dogs in loving homes? In the appendixes located at the back of this book, you will find lists of national purebred rescue chairmen (virtually every American Kennel Club [AKC] breed is represented), Greyhound rescues (both at dog tracks and through nonprofit organizations), and contact points for humane organizations. Every rescue program I have ever come in contact with was always run on a very tight budget, so monetary donations are always appreciated. Other services and supplies in demand are volunteer time, foster home care, supplies, pet food, transportation, educational materials, and obedience training skills. If you want to help, any assistance will be greatly appreciated and you will come away with a good feeling every day of having contributed to saving a dog's life.

In a perfect world, there would be no unwanted dogs. However, as long as there are people who care and dogs that love, we'll make a dent somehow.

Forgotten

By Lani A. George

Cold fingers of rain drip from matted fur.
Scabs cling, half-on, half-off.
He slows to a walk and stops to lap from
a puddle, the oil rainbow sliding around his tongue
in the black of the street.
His muzzle is flecked with gray, his teeth a little worn.
He slowly sniffs the air and moves on.

A red velvet ribbon lies in a bag of foil and tinsel.
He stops, and for a moment, remembers:

a day when his fur was burnished gold and he was warm.
A day when he was wrapped in ribbon under a tree
with lights and laughter. A day when he was hugged
so gently in a child's arms and kissed.

He remembers
and moves on,
his gait a little slower,
his eyes a little dimmer.
His gaze shifts to a home off the street. He strains
and sees tawny paws and a little black nose
pressed against the glow of the window,
remnants of a ribbon hanging from puppy teeth.

His tail wags once. The puppy's body wiggles in the window.
Then he turns and walks away,
and the night swallows him and does not remember.

CHAPTER 1
The Advantages (and Challenges) of Buying an Adult Dog

So, you think you might like to adopt an adult dog? Perhaps you've read the statistics put out by the American Humane Association on the numbers of unwanted dogs in the United States. Or, maybe you've seen a documentary on the plight of the racing Greyhound. Or, possibly you bumped into someone who runs a purebred rescue organization. At any rate, you're interested. And that's great. I hope as you read through this book you'll come away inspired, educated and ready to choose the perfect preowned pet for your family.

The Advantages

Adopting or buying an adult dog has a lot going for it; unfortunately, not everyone thinks about this option when they are considering buying a dog. I know I didn't. Years ago, when I had to put my first Whippet, Barrister's Silver Trinket, C.D. to sleep due to uterine cancer at the young age of eight, I was planning to purchase another puppy. My parents, however, gently persuaded me to take in a 5-year-old male from their kennels named "Moe." (Yes, named after one of the Three Stooges.) Moe was a stunning fawn and white, male Whippet that wasn't quite good enough for the show ring and a smidgeon too slow to be competitive in racing. Mom and Dad thought he'd make a great housepet and encouraged me to give him a try. They were right.

Moe was a constant companion, curling up in the front seat of my convertible wherever I traveled, sleeping in front of my nightstand every night (I offered the bed, but he preferred the nightstand), and loving me unconditionally. After Moe passed away, in his sleep at the age of 15, I was hooked on adult dogs. Through the years, my "adult dog" list has grown to include many, many loving memories. To be honest, I have become so spoiled by the ease of taking in an adult dog and by the minimal turmoil it creates in my life, that I really don't know if I'll ever get a puppy again!

1

Obviously, there are many advantages to adopting an adult dog; but, in case you haven't thought of all of them yourself yet, here's a handy list:

1. *What you see is what you get*
When you adopt an adult dog, you immediately know a lot about the dog's physical attributes. As an adult, the dog's size, confirmation and coat aren't going to change.

This knowledge is particularly important if the dog involved is a mixed breed. How often have we seen ads in the paper for backyard accidents that involve unusual crosses? And who could possibly guess the outcome of such strange blendings as a collie-rottweiler mix or a lab-boxer combination? The puppies may look cute but . . . the puppy owner has no clue as to how that dog is going to develop. In fact, the owner of the puppies may not even know for certain what the mix really is. (Dr. Jekyll may very well grow into Mr. Hyde within a matter of months.)

Adopting or buying an adult dog takes the guesswork out of the "mixed" equation. You'll know if the dog is going to grow up to look like Lassie with an attitude or, in the case of the lab-boxer mix, perhaps a heavyset, red-brindle.

You'll also be able to tell whether the dog has a long or short coat. Because the coat length is not obvious when the dog is a puppy, many puppy owners simply don't understand or don't fully appreciate the amount of time, money and care that goes into some types of coats. With mixed breeds, the type of coat itself might be a surprise to the puppy owner. In the example of the collie-rottweiler cross, the puppies might have appeared to look all the same, but some may grow rather thick, long coats while others wouldn't. With an adult dog, you won't be fooled into thinking that you're buying a shorthaired, low-maintenance type of dog and then wind up with the canine equivalent of a wooly mammoth.

2. *Congenital conditions/diseases are more readily discernable*
Another important advantage of buying or adopting an adult dog is that many common diseases and maladies can be detected in adult dogs but not in puppies! Countless puppy owners have been crushed with the news that their prized possession does not have "clear hips" and will, over time, be crippled by hip dysplasia. Depending on the age of the dog, veterinarians can test for such things as vision and hearing problems, congenital heart disease, and hip dysplasia.

3. Chewing is less of a problem

How many puppy owners have you seen grimacing about the latest $100 pair of shoes the puppy used as an after dinner mint or the leg of the dining room table that was used as a substitute chew toy? The fact is that puppies cut teeth and during this phase of their lives, they need to chew a lot. On the other hand, adult dogs have all their teeth in place and don't have the same needs to chew. This is not to say that an adult dog won't find a plush toy particularly fun to rip up (our Greyhound, Soxie, did that) or that it won't chew a seat belt in half while waiting for you to return out of the grocery store (Pete, another one of our Greyhounds, was the guilty party here). It just means that the sometimes frantic need to chew caused by the eruption of new teeth is not present in adult dogs. In other words, you're one step ahead of the game.

4. Adults dogs can be spayed/neutered immediately

Another benefit of owning an adult dog is that the dog has reached maturation and can be immediately spayed or neutered. You don't have to wait until your puppy reaches maturity at six months to a year or more. You don't have to worry about your male puppy failing to fill out because it was neutered too soon. In fact, you may not have to worry about spay/neuter at all with an adult dog. Many (but obviously not enough!) dog owners are automatically neutering their pet animals. It's a good idea.

5. Activity level is determinable

Do hyperactive dogs drive you crazy? Or are you looking for a dog that keeps going, and going, and going? With an adult dog you can generally get a very good sense of not only the dog's activity level but also the dog's exercise requirements. With a puppy, you can't always do this. When a couch-potato German Shorthaired Pointer (GSP) female is bred to a fantastic "field" GSP, what kind of puppy are you going to get? If the pup is active as a youngster, will it continue along this route? Or will it settle down at 12 months, two years or not until it's ready to pass onto the next world? Adult dogs are generally calmer and a little less active than their juvenile counterparts, but an active dog could still drive an owner nuts (if the owner doesn't want an active dog). By selecting an adult dog, you have a better feeling for what you're getting yourself into. You'll know whether you'll need to jog five miles a day with the dog, go for long walks several times a day, let it run hard for ten minutes in an enclosed field, or just turn on a good soap opera and let the dog "veg" on the recliner.

6. You'll have a leg up, so to speak, on housebreaking

An adult dog also has better control over its bladder and other bodily functions than a puppy. (Hurray!!) Once your new dog gets acclimated and on a regular feeding schedule, you won't have to walk it every hour or so, as you might a puppy. You also won't have to worry about the dribbles that occur when a young pup gets excited. An adult dog should be able to sleep through the entire night (again, once it's on a good schedule) without begging you to let it out in the wee hours of the morning.

Another benefit, is that many adult dogs come housebroken or at least crate trained. You may have to teach the new dog that your house is a house, but at least you've got a gigantic head start. And even if the dog isn't housebroken, the adult dog's capacity to learn housebreaking is much greater than a puppy's. Generally speaking, the housebreaking training is a little easier and generally goes much faster with an adult dog.

7. Old dogs can learn new tricks

Adult dogs actually have an advantage over the little guys. With puppies, one of the greatest challenges in training is simply getting the pup's attention. If you've ever attended a puppy kindergarten class, you'll know what I'm talking about. Treats, clickers, toys, squeakies and lots and lots of enthusiasm still sometimes aren't enough to get a youngster's undivided attention for more than a split second. With adults, this task is much easier. In fact, some adult dogs come already knowing how to follow through on some basic commands.

8. General temperament can be determined

Generally speaking, an adult dog's temperament is fairly well-formed. If the dog is dominant-aggressive, you (or an experienced dog person) should be able to determine that undesirable trait immediately. Likewise, if the dog is extremely fearful, that, too, can be readily detected. And, if the dog is like most of the 52.5 million pet dogs in this country, it may have its quirks, but overall, it's pretty loveable.

9. Abilities and aptitude are visible.

Do you want to hunt with your dog? Backpack on the weekends? Play flyball or compete in agility events? Or are you looking for a canine that would enjoy serving in an animal-assisted therapy program? If you are seeking out a special dog for a particular purpose, many times there is less chance of error in choosing an adult dog. The dog's health, strength, athletic ability, temperament, aptitude toward learning, and other qualities can be more easily determined than with an 8-week-old puppy.

10. More adaptable to 9-5ers.

A puppy cannot be left alone all day. For those professionals and dual-income families in which no one is home during working hours, a puppy is going to get into lots of trouble. Housebreaking is extremely difficult as is trying to find the time and energy after a long day at the office to socialize, habitualize and train the young pup.

An adult dog would, of course, prefer to have someone home all day with it (and some breeds demand it). However, if a dog must be left alone while you're off working, an adult dog will generally fare much better than a puppy. With the help of a noontime walk from a neighbor or pet-sitter, or a dog door from an "indestructible" area of the house out to a securely, fenced yard, an adult dog can many times adapt much better to this lifestyle than a youngster. (Caution: Don't think you can skimp on the daily obedience training!)

The Challenges

If anyone tries to tell you that adult dogs are perfect in every way and you'll never have a day's problem with them, red flags should be waving in your head and you should be hearing alarms, bells and whistles!! There is no such thing as a perfect dog, except for all the dogs I have owned, of course. Every dog has its pluses and minuses. In a follow-up study to Petronek's work on dogs turned into shelters, Petronek found that (not surprisingly) the behavior profiles of the relinquished dogs were the same as the behavior profiles of the dogs once they were adopted. In other words, if the dog was dropped off because it wasn't housebroken, a short stay at the pound wasn't going to miraculously "solve" anything. It is up to the adoptive owners to 1) take the time to work with the dog to make it a good citizen, and 2) teach the dog what it does not know.

Some people are more capable of working through some of the behavior problems than others. For example, there are those dog people who are very good at obedience training. For them, a boisterous, unruly lab may not be a particular challenge. After a week of regular training, the dog might be a new canine. For others without the time or training experience, this same dog might be a nightmare. Another example might be a dog that has a known history of chasing cats. For a person with no other pets, caring for the adopted dog would be a breeze. However, for a person with several cats, the behavior modification training necessary to get all creatures to live together in harmony might be overwhelming (and possibly fruitless).

So, if you know you don't have the experience or patience to deal with certain problems, by all means try to avoid them. And most importantly, be educated as to what kinds of problems might exist with an adult dog. If you have the ability to identify a dog's challenges (i.e., know what you're getting into), you can better weigh the dog's challenges against its advantages before making your selection.

The following are some of the most frequently heard concerns of people considering adopting an adult dog:

1. Unknown past

How do you know if the adult you are considering adopting was socialized properly as a pup during its formative period? What if the dog was abused? Neglected? How will this affect the dog's temperament today? Studies have shown that a dog's life experiences - particularly as a puppy - definitely shapes the dog's temperament. Fortunately, however, what you see is what you get. Dogs don't generally try to hide their evil sides; if they've got one, you (or an experienced dog person) should be able to see it. If they're timid, you'll know. Given enough time with a dog, a person should be able to glean not only a lot about the dog's temperament, but also its likes, dislikes, phobias, and fears.

What if the person dropping off the dog to a shelter or breed rescue organization fills out a form as to why the dog didn't work out but lies, thinking that the dog will have a better chance of finding a home? If you are very concerned that the dog must have been dropped off for some dreadful reason, don't be. In general, studies have shown that most dogs are disposed of NOT because they bite, have strange quirks or are considered otherwise unsafe (breeders, rescues, dog tracks and shelters typically euthanize any dog with a history of aggression or biting), but rather because the dog has simply become inconvenient.

So, who gets turned into shelters? Untrained, boisterous Golden Retrievers fall into this category. Great Danes and other giant breeds that eat much more than their owners anticipated might also be candidates for desertion. Old English Sheepdogs and other longhaired breeds that shed constantly may be perceived by a lazy owner as too much work. A Jack Russell Terrier that is very active could have driven its prior owner batty.

A mixed-breed that tends to run away could have been a problem for someone with no fenced yard. Dogs whose owners either didn't have the time or money to care for them or didn't want to make the effort to correct naughty habits are the dogs you will generally find up for adoption.

Sometimes aggressive or unpredictable dogs do find their way into shelters, so do be careful and never adopt a dog that you might have the slightest apprehension about. (See the section on aggression in Chapter 7.) There are far too many loving, even-tempered dogs to risk serious injury with one that is not.

2. *Unknown Breeding*

How can you tell if the parents of a dog were well-bred, healthy breed specimens - or poorly-bred backyard dogs prone to various congenital diseases? Most likely you can't. With an adult dog, especially a mix, a person can usually only guess at the dog's heritage. However, the quality of dogs in shelters, dog tracks and with rescue groups might surprise you.

Shelters and rescues: Many times a person will have paid hundreds and hundreds of dollars for the prestige of owning a purebred and then dumped the dog off unceremoniously at the pound a year later along with its champion-studded pedigree. There are also purebred dogs available for adoption that are the result of backyard breedings, puppy mills and pet shop purchases. These dogs may be AKC registered, but are not what you'd call "well-bred," meaning that the breeders were in the game for profit only and were not selectively breeding for health, temperament and confirmation.

And then you'll find the "American" dogs that are usually the result of careless dog ownership. Mixed breeds generally outnumber their purebred counterparts in the pound with anywhere from equal numbers to a 3:1 ratio. And, not surprisingly, the majority of mixes aren't the unrecognizable melting pots of the past; according to Project BREED. Rather, the majority are half-breeds of a purebred.

Dog tracks and Greyhound placement services (rescues): You'll find few if any problems with the dogs. The typical track dog is healthy, robust, sinewy and extremely intelligent. The only reason these fine animals are up for adoption is that they are running 41 mph when everyone else is running 42 mph. (See Chapter 6: Dog Tracks and the Retired Greyhound: A Special Case.)

In general, you may not be able to know exactly what the dog's breeding is, but if you study up on your dog breeds and understand general behaviors, potential diseases and disorders, you'll at least know what to look for in your adopted dog. As I mentioned earlier, by the time a dog reaches adulthood, there are so many things that can be readily determined, such as health, confirmation, coat, activity level and temperament, that the risk of the adoption is more evenly balanced with the information that is readily available to you.

3. Untrained

An untrained, fully-grown dog can be a handful. "St. Bernard puppies are probably one of the most adorable in the world," comments Carol Varner Beck, owner of Star's Saints and chairperson of the St. Bernard Club of America's national rescue organization."So, people think it's cute when their fuzzy little puppy jumps up on them." She adds seriously, "It's not cute when a 180-lb St. Bernard does the same thing." In large breeds such as the St. Bernard and in strong breeds such as Labrador and Golden Retrievers, life can be difficult until the dog is appropriately trained. In these instances, the adopter must be ready to take on the immediate responsibility of training their new dog to become a respectable member of the family.

4. Un-housebroken

Fully-grown dogs make bigger "mistakes" when they make them than puppies do. Sometimes males are in the habit of marking their territory or simply watering anything that looks like it might be a bush, shrub or tree. I am reminded of an occasion in which I was out one afternoon with Pete, my 80-lb Greyhound, and came home to find my husband and son had been busy setting up a little Christmas tree. Even though the dog and I had been out for quite some time and Pete's urges had been completely taken care of, he walked right up to that little ornament laden tree, sniffed it and proceeded to water it right in front of our eyes. At the time, Pete had been completely housebroken and accident free for nearly a year. However, we had never introduced him to a Christmas tree. We learned our lesson and he learned his. (But he can still be seen looking wistfully every time we bring home a large tropical plant or set up our annual tree.) Adult dogs are generally easier and takes less time to housebreak than a puppy; however, the owner must be dedicated to getting the job done or it could be a very costly endeavor.

5. Unsocialized

Some dogs have not had a great opportunity to meet many people. The typical dog that runs through the adoption system has had some socialization and just needs some tender, loving care to become a gregarious, fun-loving sort. However, there are those dogs, and they are generally in the minority, that have been neglected or suffered through extreme situations, making them leery of most people. Dogs that have been caged for many months or years, such as brood bitches at puppy mills, often fall into this category. If the dog fears humans, there is the potential to have a volatile situation on hand. Dogs that need improvement with their socialization skills may require extensive work. Only owners who are extremely patient and have extensive experience with dogs should consider working with a dog such as this. Fearful dogs are not recommended for people with children. Fear biting can be a serious problem.

6. Unhabitualized

What happens when you put a city slicker on a farm? Or try to confine a free-roaming soul in a high-rise apartment? (We're talking dogs here . . .) Your house, your car, your routine, even your neighborhood will probably all be strange and new to your adopted dog. Retired Greyhounds have to be taught to go up and down stairs (they don't have those at the race track).

A Boxer may not know that the vacuum cleaner isn't going to suck him up. A mixed-breed may be fearful of the toilet flushing.

Some dogs take less than 24-hours to adjust to their new surroundings. Others may take much longer.

Mary Powell, rescue coordinator for the Blossom Valley Beagle Club in Sunnyvale, California, often receives Beagles from laboratories. "These beagles range from one and half to six or seven years old and have never experienced anything outside of the lab," says Powell. "They've never seen grass, been out in the sunshine or felt a breeze. It's like taking a puppy whose eyes have just opened and introducing them to the world." Powell says that at first the beagles try to cower or hide in their crates, "but we don't let them." Powell, with the help of many dedicated club members, put the lab beagles through a sort of rehab program with lots of petting, handling, and careful introduction to all the "scary" things of life as a pet. "After two to three months, we have a bunch of happy little beagles."

How long your adopted dog takes to adjust depends on the extent of their fear and uncertainty and your patience and gentleness in helping them overcome their trepidations.

Adult dogs are a win-win situation

As you have probably picked up, it is my strong feeling that the benefits of adopting an adult dog far outweigh any challenges that might occur. The key to success, however, is going into the relationship with your eyes open. You must: 1) have a thorough understanding of the various challenges you might encounter, 2) outline in your mind which of these challenges you are willing to take on and steer clear of those that are more than you can handle, 3) realize the level of commitment necessary to overcome the challenges you are willing to accept, and 4) dedicate yourself to making the dog a permanent part of your family.

Kids & Dogs: Like Bread & Butter

"Let's explode this myth right now that dogs and children automatically know how to act around each other," says Wayne Hunthausen, D.V.M., director of Animal Behavior Consultations at Westwood Animal Hospital, past president of the American Veterinary Society of Animal Behavior and author of the video: Dogs, Cats and Kids: Learning to Be Safe Around Animals (Pet Love Partnership, LP: 1996). "In most cases, you have to teach dogs about kids. And you have to teach children how to interact with dogs. Dogs and kids must both know what their boundaries in the relationship are and what each other likes and dislikes." With a shelter dog, Hunthausen advises parents to "assume there's a problem until you determine otherwise."

When the child is younger than four years of age, additional problems are posed by adopting a dog. Hunthausen explains, "A parent must be capable of providing 24-hour supervision until the child is four years old or so. Or, the parent must be able to separate the dog from the infant or toddler at all times." The problems arise not only from dominance, possessive and fear aggression - but also from the sheer size ratio of dog to child. Hunthausen adds that, "A big, unruly dog can be every bit as dangerous to a little child as a dog that bites."

"If you have little children, choosing a dog from a shelter is fraught with peril. You're just asking for trouble," emphasizes Barbara Sgambellone, Animal Adoption & Rescue Foundation, Inc. (AARF) of Winston-Salem, N.C. "At AARF, we won't place a dog in a home with a child under the age of four. We also won't place little dogs with small children. All it takes is one minute, one bite and a dog can ruin a lifetime. I advise people just to wait until their children are a little older."

The word is, proceed with great caution and anticipate trouble. Many parents swear by shelter dogs and have had great luck. My personal advice to parents of very small children is to go through a purebred rescue, a breeder, or shelter at which the dog has received a temperament evaluation and has been fostered and/or closely observed for some time. In other words, adopt a dog that is a known entity. Don't take chances! In addition, be sure to work with your children at a very early age to teach them to be kind and considerate to animals. And, never take your eyes off your child and the dog. If you can't supervise, separate.

CHAPTER 2
Is Dog Ownership for You?

Assessing your situation honestly

Dog ownership is not for everyone. There are countless times when a person wanted to do the right thing. He or she adopted an animal only to find that they themselves were not capable of providing the level of care necessary for a dog to be happy. Dogs, like young children, provide unconditional love, but they're also high maintenance.

Before you make an impulsive adoption, carefully assess your situation. If you decide that dog ownership is not going to work out for you right now, don't adopt a dog and don't feel bad. There are so many other ways you can help! However, if dog ownership is a real possibility for you, then read on! The following are some areas of dog ownership that should be considered before making the commitment to adopt an adult dog.

Financial

Many people are under the misconception that an adopted dog is cheap. After all, it is quite easy to pick up a mix from the shelter for $25 - $75. However, the common adage that the purchase price is the least expensive part of the deal is so true with dogs. The adoption fee is just the beginning! The actual estimated cost of owning an average (40-lb) dog is between $500-$700 a year. The following list includes just a few of the expenses a dog owner may incur.

Spay/Neuter

If you're adopting an adult dog it should be with the intention of saving the dog's life, not perpetuating the problem of overpopulation. Most adoption sources will require a spay/neuter to be completed before or immediately after the paperwork is signed and the dog is released to you.

Depending on the area of the country, prices may vary but there are few places that will spay a dog for less than $100 (slightly less for a neuter). There are some nonprofit organizations whose sole purpose is to help people pay for spay/neuters. It may be well worth your while to check into this option.

Routine veterinary care

Every dog requires an annual veterinarian visit, inoculations (rabies, boosters, etc.), tests for heartworms and other parasites, along with other necessary veterinary expenses, such as a kennel cough vaccination (applied nasally). Then there's worming medicine (if your dog has picked up worms), monthly heartworm pills (the heavier the dog, the more expensive the dosage), and flea and tick preventive medication (quite costly). A dog owner can expect to pay at least $200 a year in veterinary care and preventive medicine for a healthy, happy dog with no problems.

Special "rescue"""care

Some adopted dogs may initially require more extensive veterinary care or exams than others. In many areas of the country, testing positive on a heartworm test is not uncommon for a rescued dog. If the dog you choose has heartworm, you may find that the curative treatment of heartworm is expensive. It can also be risky for some breeds and older dogs and the decision to treat must be weighed with the extent of the infestation. Dogs that have been running wild for several days or weeks may be severely infested with fleas, ticks and mange. These dogs may require more veterinary care than a good dip. Some dogs may require dental work. Rotted or broken teeth may need to be removed or repaired. X-rays may be necessary to test for hip dysplasia. The list goes on.

If you are adopting your dog from a breeder, breed rescue or dog track, you probably won't have to worry too much about special care risks since the dog will have been screened for most of this before you take it home. Some well-financed shelters also have dogs vet checked and cleared of serious problems prior to offering the dog; however, many don't.

Emergency care

If something is going to happen to your dog, it will happen either just before you are to leave on a trip, while you are traveling with or without the dog, or in the dead of night. (With my dogs, timing is everything.) All of these scenarios mean that you cannot take the dog to your regular veterinarian during regular hours, but instead will have to pay a premium for off-hours assistance or the services of an emergency care center. These options, though extremely valuable, are not inexpensive. Last Christmas, two out-of-state, after hours visits to the emergency room totaled more than $300. The injured body part was a toe.

According to Dr. Marsha Wallace, national chairperson of the English Cocker Spaniel Club of America Rescue Program, she commonly hears lack of money for veterinarian bills as an excuse to turn in a dog. "We see dogs turned in because the owners can't afford the vet bills. The dog will have one illness and they'll say 'I don't have money for the vet bill.'" Since emergencies are always unplanned, Wallace recommends that anyone considering dog ownership should set aside money just for veterinary expenses. "A dog owner should be able to have $500 available at any given time to cover vet bills."

Grooming

Can you clip your own dog's toenails once a month, or will you have to pay for a groomer or your veterinarian to do it? Can you bathe your dog regularly, or will you have to pay someone else to do this job? And probably most importantly, do you know what to do if your dog's coat requires special care?

Generally, coat types fall into one of three categories: 1) true, low maintenance coats--shorthaired coats that require a simple brushing every once in a while; 2) the "you-think-this-coat's-gonna-be-easy-but-it's-really-not" coats--members of this group are shorthaired dogs that shed a lot or dogs that appear to be shorthaired but really are well-groomed medium to longhaired dogs (English Cocker Spaniels, Schnauzers, etc.); and 3) the "exotic" coats--one look at these longhaired dogs and you know you're going to be spending time brushing, trimming, clipping, thinning, shaving, or (indirectly) sending your local groomer's children to college.

A common misconception is that low maintenance coats do not require any attention. Not true. These coats are more forgiving; you won't get mats, hot spots or other nasty hair and skin problems because you missed a brushing or two or three. However, daily care is preferable (those brushings feel so good).

Medium to longhaired coats definitely require daily attention. A quick brush down before bedtime or after a walk may be all that's necessary - but it is necessary. Some coats, such as the longhaired St. Bernard, require the owner to learn special brushing techniques. Then there are the high-maintenance coats that require special combinations of grooming techniques. For example, an Afghan Hound - in order to look its best - requires a combination of brushing and clipping. Other breeds are more complex; the Puli requires the owner to cord the dog's entire coat. (Not a job for amateurs!). A mixed-breed that is a descendant of a "high-maintenance" breed may need special grooming, too. For a small dog, the bill usually isn't too bad - $30 or so every six to eight weeks. Large breeds are more expensive.

And a final note on coats, all dogs shed. There is no such thing as a dog that doesn't lose its old hair and replace it with new hair. The old hair falls out on your floors, couches and beds. The new hair grows in quickly so it can fall out, too, and rejoin its fallen comrades. It's a never ending cycle. If the dog has a short, thin coat - it stands to reason that it has less hair to lose and therefore will be less of a problem. If on the other hand, the dog's coat is thick, long, or that beautiful short, thin coat grows in quickly, you'll notice more hair about the house. With daily brushing, the shedding is minimized, unless you've chosen a dog that grows a tremendous winter coat. In this instance, spring and fall can be difficult seasons.

Food

Usually the cost of food is not an issue with most dog owners, but it can be. High quality dog food, which is what you want to feed your dog, usually runs around $25 or more for a 40-pound bag. For the little Dachshund that eats 2/3 cup a day, feeding is very inexpensive. For the Great Dane that packs away eight or more heaping cups, the cost of the food bill - along with the chew bones, smoked pigs' ears and dog biscuits, of course, could add up quickly.

Another item people generally forget to consider is the expense of special diets. If your dog has one or more of many possible health problems, you may have to feed it a prescription diet.

Therefore, just because your dog weighs in at slightly more than 10 pounds, doesn't necessarily mean that your food bill will be low. A diminutive dog with a digestive disorder may be quite costly to its owner.

Equipment

Most everybody realizes that they will need to purchase a collar and a leash. Beyond that, many people are a little foggy about the other necessary expenditures. Your dog will need a comfy dog bed, possibly a dog house, a properly fitted crate, a water and food bowl, a container to store your dog's food in, and of course, your grooming supplies: toe nail clipper, brushes, shampoos and conditioners. A healthy supply of enzyme-eating carpet cleaner is a good idea, too.

As you assess your home and lifestyle, you may find you need additional supplies, such as baby gates, dog barriers for the car, dog doors and fencing.

Training classes

Don't forget to include obedience classes in your dog budget. This is a "must have" expense for a successful dog placement! You'll get a very high rate of return from this investment, guaranteed.

Classes range anywhere from $35 for an eight-week basic obedience group session to $20 an hour or more for private lessons. Being personally involved in the obedience training is best because you are being trained along with the dog! If you don't have time to train the dog yourself, your expenses will be even greater to have someone train your canine for you. Be prepared to do whatever it takes!

Dog walking

If you are a dual-income family, there may be no one home over the lunch hour to care for the dog. Are you prepared to pay a pet sitter $10 to $15 a day to walk your dog and play with it for a half hour? Or can you arrange for a trustworthy neighbor to perform these chores? A dog can't be expected to "last" nine or more hours a day without being able to relieve itself. Even if you do have a dog that could win the bladder marathon, it's just not healthy for the dog to ask it to wait that long during its active hours. A walk every four hours is ideal or the ability to go in and out into a fenced yard as the dog pleases maybe even better.

Boarding kennels

If you travel often, kennel fees can really add up. Small dogs may be only $8 a day, but medium to larger breeds (more than 50 pounds) can cost $15 or more a day. When the family is taking a vacation to Disneyworld, you've got enough expenses. Can you also afford the $210 bill for a wo-week vacation? Or the $420 bill for two dogs? Be sure to take your travel schedule into consideration along with your finances (or the lack thereof) before adopting a dog.

Carpet, couches and expensive furniture

"I used to own a white couch," seems to be the hallmark comment made by devoted dog owners. Invariably this statement is accompanied by a laugh and a shake of the head. It's only funny now because the couch is in the distant past. I can vouch for the fact that it's not too amusing when the situation is in the present. Even with regular baths, dogs do not do well on white furniture or white carpets, for that matter. You will either have to make your dog understand that the furniture is off limits, or resign yourself to camouflage fabrics, frequent cleanings, heavy Scotch guarding and an occasional reupholstering.

Family

If you are a single person living alone, you don't have to ask anyone's permission to buy a dog.

However, if you are married, live with other adults, and/or have children, it's another story.

Men

If you want a dog and your wife doesn't, don't buy the dog anyway and expect your spouse to take care of it while you're at work. Guess where your prized pooch is going to end up? If it's untrained and your spouse perceives the canine to be an intolerable inconvenience, more than likely the hapless canine will spend its days locked up in the basement or thrown out in the backyard. And then your spouse will complain (and maybe the neighbors will, too) that the dog barks constantly. Make sure the decision to adopt a dog is a joint one and that both partners are willing to equally share the responsibilities and joys of dog ownership.

Women

Before adopting a dog, very carefully consider your time restraints. If you work all day and have two children in day care, are you going to be able to give everyone the attention they need when you come home from work each day? You'll have two children clamoring for your love, homework to get through, dinner to make (hey, even frozen dinners involve opening a box!), and a dog that needs 20-minutes of obedience training or a 30-minute walk. Can you fit all this into your schedule? For single parents or women with husbands who work very late or are on the second-shift, adding a dog to the hectic schedule may be the straw that breaks the camel's back.

Adults Living At Home

For a variety of reasons many young adults, and even those in their 30s , are still living at home with their parents. If this is your situation, you MUST include your parents in your decision to adopt a dog. In fact, most good adoption agencies will require your parents to be part of the interview process and will insist on their support of the new dog before they will place a canine with you. There's good reason for this, too. You are in your parents' home and like it or not you ultimately live by their rules. Just like when you were in grade school, if your parents said "no" that meant no. Also, stop for a minute and consider who will be caring for the dog while you are at work - or off skiing for the weekend with friends. If your parents don't want a dog, your relationship will be strained and their attention to the dog and its needs will be minimal. Don't do this to your parents - or to your dog. Either get your parents' whole-hearted support - or wait until you can get your own place!

Adults Living With Roommates

In this situation, it is extremely important to get the support and approval of everyone who lives with you. If you don't, one of several scenarios will develop: 1) your roommates will force you to return the dog, 2) if you refuse to return the dog, your roommates will force you to find a new abode, or 3) the dog could be severely mistreated or "let loose" in your absence. Don't strain your relationship with your roommates (unless you're looking for a reason to move out and even then there are other ways to do this!). Involve everyone who will have contact with the dog in the dog adoption process.

Parents of Older Children

Don't adopt a dog expecting to teach your children "responsibility." The dog is YOUR responsibility! As a parent, you are the primary caregiver and keeper of the peace. There's no problem with assigning your older children the duties of feeding, brushing or "yard patrolling" the dog as long as you vigilantly check up to make sure the chore is accomplished in a timely manner. The dog should never suffer because of the forgetfulness of a child.

Parents of Young Children

Not every dog is Lassie! If you are the parent of a baby, toddler or preschooler, are you prepared to NEVER EVER leave your young child alone with the dog? As the parent of two young children, I can testify that this can be a rather daunting and exhausting task. Tail pulling, ear twisting, eye poking, leg biting, foot stomping are all things a little child will try to do to your dog. Plus, you have to be extremely organized to schedule in the dog's regular walks (particularly if you don't have a fenced yard) around nap times, meal times and snack times. If your dog needs to go out and you're rocking the baby to sleep, you can't be mad if you find a "present" waiting for you. If you don't think you're up to the task, then do yourself a tremendous favor and wait until your children are older and more controllable and your life has regained a little normalcy to it.

Adult Children of Elderly Parents

Dogs are wonderful therapy for the aging. However, if you are providing care for an aging, frail parent in your home, you may also want to consider the potential hazards a new dog may present.

Little dogs may get underfoot and cause a fall. Large, exuberant canines may have a tendency to bowl people over. Some elderly people are fearful of dogs. When making the decision to purchase a dog, please take the feelings and concerns of all family members into consideration.

Lifestyle

Dogs love their human pack. To them, being around people all day is pleasurable. So, it stands to reason that the ideal situation for a dog would be either to go to work every day with you, or have someone (you or someone else really fun) stay at home all day with the dog. Most dog owners will not fall into either of these categories. But that doesn't mean dog ownership is "out" for you. It just means that you have to be willing to make the necessary changes and financial sacrifices to make your situation ideal for the dog.

Those who aren't at home

Leaving your dog outside all day is generally not a good alternative. In most areas of this country, there are weather conditions that are dangerous for the dog's health: Winters in the northern states are quite bitter and summers just about everywhere get pretty hot.

In addition, a dog that is left out all day will generally do one of three things: 1) get bored and dig up everything in the yard; 2) get bored and jump the fence; or 3) get bored and bark nonstop until you come home. The first scenario will only serve to increase your blood pressure, though your landscaper may enjoy the repeat business. The second scenario will cause any dog owner's heart to skip a beat and begin a frantic and many times fruitless search. The third scenario will annoy the neighbors and may cause people to start leaving you nasty notes.

So, what can you do? No, letting your dog have the run of the house is not the answer either. Eight or nine hours is much too long for a dog to go without relieving itself during its active period. Additionally, you may come home to find your favorite couch shredded, the blinds pulleddown and many inedible objects gone. (Guess where they went?) If you can "dog proof" a room such as a laundry room or kitchen and put in a dog door out to a fenced back yard, you've got a great option. The dog can go in and out at will. This freedom in no way guarantees that your dog won't dig, jump or bark, but at least the severity of the weather won't ever be a concern and your house is relatively safe from canine danger.

Another option is to crate your dog during the day and have a pet sitter or neighbor come over once or twice a day to let your dog out to exercise, play and relieve itself. This method guarantees that nothing in your house will ever be destroyed while you are gone and that the dog will never get over the fence, dig up the petunias or bark its little head off. However, it does restrict your dog's movements during the day, so a properly-fitted, roomy crate is absolutely essential. And, if you hire the services of a pet sitter, you must be prepared to fork over more than $8 to $12 a visit. If you work very long hours and require two visits a day, five days a week, 50 weeks out of the year, that's roughly $5,000 in pet sitting/ dog walking fees.

Those who travel frequently

How many days in the month are you gone from your job? If you travel a lot, you'll need to figure out the expenses and logistics of boarding your dog. From a monetary standpoint alone, frequent fliers with financial concerns might seriously consider a small (or smaller) dog.

Boarding rates are usually based on the weight of the dog, with a large dog's rates being double to triple that of a small dog.

Those who move often

We live in a very mobile society with many vocations requiring frequent moves. Employees of the military, some government agencies, and many transportation companies often relocate every two to three years. Laborers may find themselves following the job market. Executives may hopscotch the country while climbing the corporate ladder. Typically, we take these moves in stride. But many times bringing along our dogs can be extremely inconvenient, not to mention expensive.

When Jim Shields, a naval officer, and his wife, Elizabeth, were scheduled for an overseas tour, they didn't panic. At the time, they owned a rescued collie and a cocker spaniel. Instead of giving up their beloved canines for adoption, as many, less dedicated people have been known to do, the young couple made arrangements to fly their two dogs with them to Italy. Once in Italy, the Shields' discovered that they couldn't get a decent quality dog food from the area stores. The couple arranged to have fresh, high quality food shipped in from the United States on a regular basis. Committed dog owners, the Shields did whatever it took to keep their "family' together and healthy. This is the personal commitment everyone who moves must be prepared to take.

Those who rent

I have a personal story to tell on this one. A few years ago, my husband, Randy, was notified that we would have to move to the D.C. area. We had less than a month to find a new home for our two small children and dog. Since we knew this move would only be for no more than five or six years, we asked the realtor to pull up rentals.

At a meeting with the agent, we were given a two-inch tall stack of computer printouts. "We have more than 80 townhouses on the market in the school district you requested," explained the realtor. "Where do you want to start?"

"Well, I'd like a place near a tot lot for the kids," I explained. The realtor sifted through the stack, ripping pages off and handing us a thick stack. I added rather nonchalantly, "Oh yes, and we do have a dog."

The realtor stopped. She tried to maintain her composure. After a pause, she smiled and laughed, "Well, that will actually simplify matters." She quickly went through the stack and handed us less than a dozen options.

Randy was the first to speak, "It says here: 'twenty pound limit.'" He looked up at the realtor. "Do they really mean that? Or is it negotiable?"

The realtor smiled sweetly (because she really was a sweet person), "Well, how big is your dog?"

Our answer of 80 pounds probably wasn't the one she wanted to hear.

To make a long story short, only two rentals would consider a dog that weighed more than 20 pounds and both required at least two letters of recommendation from neighbors stating what wonderful dog owners we were and how well-behaved our dog was. The two townhouses weren't exactly what we wanted, time was running out, so we decided to buy a townhouse instead. Yes, we took on a mortgage (and they ain't cheap in Northern Virginia!) just so our 80-pound dog could come with us!

So, let this be a lesson to all renters and would-be renters: Dogs and rentals can create some additional challenges. The majority of apartments, condos, townhouses and house rentals do not allow dogs. If they do allow dogs, there is usually a weight restriction of 20 pounds. And no, there is no way you can sneak a Mastiff into your apartment without eventually getting caught. Before you are allowed to bring a dog into the rental unit, you may also be required to produce letters of good "dog ownership" to the renter. If you haven't owned a dog before, this can be difficult. And finally, many rentals that allow dogs require a deposit, sometimes quite a substantial one.

If you are a renter, be sure you check the rules and requirements first. Once you know what your limits are, be a good owner and follow them!

Level of Commitment

I am a firm believer that just about any situation can be made to work if the dog owner is creative and committed to caring for his or her dog for its lifetime. The key to making the relationship work is in recognizing your dog's needs, realizing what you will have to do to meet those needs, and committing yourself to providing your dog with a safe, happy and healthy environment. If you are willing to do whatever it takes, then you will probably make some dog, some day, a truly terrific owner.

Examples of breed purposes and how they could relate to possible home behavior.

Breed	Purpose	Possible Home Behavior
Dalmatian	Carriage dogs Protect the stables at night	Limitless energy; high activity Guard dog qualities: barking and possible biting.
Boxer	Baiting bulls, guard dog	Very active, playful, strong muscular dog that could bowl over children unintentionally.
Dachshund	Hunting dog especially bred to climb down holes after game	Digger (makes own holes) and not intimidated easily (willing to take on dogs ten times its size).
Jack Russell Terrier	Hunting fox, running into den and keeping fox at bay until the dog bolts the quarry, is dug to, or is called out by the owner.	An extremely active, intelligent, fearless dog that is neither suited for condo nor apartment life. Because the dog tends to play roughly, it is not suggested for children under five.
Labrador Retriever	Retriever	"The dog picks up everything and carries it around in its mouth . . ." Socks, shoes, magazines - all with a nice thick coating of Labrador slime.
German Shorthaired Pointer	All-purpose hunting dog High endurance Close working	Perpetual motion Always by (or under) your feet.
Shetland Sheepdog	Herding	Nipping at children to "herd" them around in the yard.
Whippet	Racing dog Hunts by sight; keen vision	Occasional sudden bursts of high velocity play followed by no movement at all. No little fuzzy thing is safe in an open field . . . especially if it moves.

CHAPTER 3
Understanding Dogs and Dog Behavior: Research Before Adopting

Steve and Cindy had always wanted a Dalmatian. One day when the couple was walking through the mall with their two small children, they spotted a Dal for sale. As the children dragged their parents to the window, Steve and Cindy's hearts melted. The young male, Pongo, seemed to be pleading and begging to go home with the family. Steve asked the shop owner if Dalmatians made good family pets. Without hesitation, the woman said, "Yes." And with that, Steve pulled out his credit card and the dog was theirs, but not for too long.

By the time Pongo had grown into an adolescent, the couple realized "what a terrible mistake they had made," relates Chris Jackson, the national rescue chairman of the Dalmatian Club of America. "When they called me, the conversation started with: 'You've got to help us.'"

* * *

One of the most common reasons a dog does not work out in a home is that the owner either did not understand dog behavior in general or was a little foggy on the peculiarities of a particular breed. Simply stated, the original owner most likely bought the dog on an emotional impulse with little knowledge or experience. Then, as the puppy matured, it suddenly began to show all sorts of natural canine behaviors and instincts. And so began the troubles . . .

In the case of Pongo, Jackson explains why a Dalmatian was the wrong breed for this youngfamily: "The mother and father both worked and had two small children. They barely had enough energy to care for their own two children, much less the energy to teach a dog the skills of living. In addition, the dog was poorly bred and had a terribly high activity level." Faced with the overwhelming job of training the unruly adolescent, the couple chose to surrender the dog to Dalmatian Rescue. Happily, Pongo found a wonderful home with a young woman who not only was experienced with Dalmatians, but also was skilled in obedience training and had the time to devote to training the young male.

So how do you avoid making the same mistake this young couple made? If you want to adopt a purebred, you can greatly increase your chances for a very successful placement by carefully researching the breed or breeds in which you are interested. If you prefer the All-American mutt, it is still important to have a well-versed background in dog behavior and an understanding of the breeds involved in your dog's mix. According to Project BREED (Breed Rescue Efforts and EDucation), Inc., more than half the dogs in animal shelters are either purebreds or "recognizable half-breed offspring." So, you'll be one step ahead by understanding at least half of your dog's ingrained behaviors! Whether you want a purebred or a mix, here are some tips to get you started.

1. The breed(s) purpose

Possibly the best piece of advice someone could receive before adopting a dog is this: Understand the purpose for which the dog was originally bred. The second most important piece of advice would then be to understand how the breed's purpose translates into "at-home" behavior.

For instance, take Pongo. Dalmatians were bred to run after carriages all day and then turn around and guard the stables at night. What does this mean for "at-home" behavior? First of all, if a dog can literally run all day, it was bred for endurance. So if you put a dog that can run all day in your home, what do you get? As a house dog, this activity level is not going to magically disappear. The dog will want to run all day inside your home. A dog with this kind of limitless energy needs to have a safe out-let to burn off a little steam. (Do you run five miles every morning and have a large backyard?)

Secondly, Dalmatians were bred to guard the stables at night. This type of work requires guard dog qualities and independent thinking. Jackson says, "The dog is not going to ask its owner if it is O.K. to bark or if it is O.K. to let someone into the barn. The dog is going to make those decisions on its own." What this means to the owner is that you've got a very intelligent, stubborn dog who, in a guarding situation, will def-initely wake the neighbors and may choose to bite.

Another example of how a breed's instinctive behaviors might affect home life could be illustrated with a Shetland Sheepdog mix. "Shelties" are herding dogs. They are very smart and very quick. With a mix involv-ing a Sheltie, don't be surprised if the dog's herding instincts come out. No problem, you say. That sounds like fun. But how fun is it going to be when your little Sheltie mix starts herding up the kids in the backyard and nips an hysterical neighbor's child? Food for thought.

Even if you think you know what a breed is like, be sure to talk to people who are heavily involved in either showing, hunting, or obedience training that breed. You might be surprised. You might also find that the dog you knew growing up as a child, for better or worse, is not the dog that is out there today. For example, the St. Bernard of 20 years ago is quite different from today's. According to Carol Varner Beck, national rescue chairperson for the St. Bernard Club of America, two decades ago the Saint had a terrible temperament. Today's Saint is truly that; a saint with an even, loving disposition.

2. Activity level

Unless you have limitless energy yourself, a "high-energy" dog is usually not a good choice for an indoor dog - and some breeds (and mixes of those breeds) are naturally more active than others. Mary Powell (Beagle Rescue) explains that despite their small size, beagles are not a good choice for apartment dwellers. "Beagles are very active and must be with people. If left alone, they will chew, bark and [outside] re-landscape your yard. They require more exercise than a Great Dane."

Within breeds there are strains - or blood lines - that are more active than others, too. In other words, if you adopt a six-year-old Labrador Retriever mix with the thought that she is going to be a tremendous "hearth" dog, you might be sorely mistaken. If the dog's lab breeding comes from field stock, she may have a relatively high activity level.

If you're adopting a purebred, find out what the breed's indoor activity level is compared with its outdoor activity level. Some breeds, such as Greyhounds, may have a high activity level outside for a brief five to ten minutes, and an extremely low (we're talking almost comatose) activity level indoors - unless you don't let them have their outside time . . . Other breeds, such as Dachshunds, may be ready to play all day - but will behave themselves until you invite them to get bouncy.

3. Two-Sided Breeds

What most people looking for a purebred don't understand is that in many breeds of dogs there are two "sides" to the breed, complete with their own set of unique characteristics. This can be a source of confusion and great consternation to the dog owner who thinks he is getting one kind of dog and ends up with a totally different kind of animal.

According to Virginia Campbell, former coordinator of the National Labrador Retriever Rescue Club and owner of the respected Campbellcroft Kennels in California, some hunting breeds (such as the Lab) can have distinct differences in confirmation and temperament between those raised to compete "in the field," and those raised to compete in the show ring. Campbell explains that the field side may be markedly more active with intense hunting instincts, whereas, the show side may be more sedate and calm. This is not to say that show dogs cannot make outstanding hunting dogs, or that field dogs cannot make good house pets. It is just a matter of what you can put up with and what is likely to drive you nuts.

"If a person buys a 'field' dog thinking they are getting a quiet, hearth dog, it could be a short-lived relationship," says Campbell. "The differences between 'field' lines and 'show' lines are distinct enough in temperament and confirmation that we [rescue] developed an information sheet with photos, comparing the two types of Labrador Retrievers." The sheet is used as an educational tool and is distributed to shelters and to prospective adopters/buyers across the country.

Other popular breeds such as Boxers have two sides, as well. According to Tracy Hendrickson, a Boxer breeder and national coordinator for Boxer Rescue, the American Boxer is "a real pussycat." However, she says there is another side to the breed: "German Boxers are a lot bigger boned and they still have the blood instinct to do Schutzhund work. Anyone who wants to do Boxers in Schutzhund, you get a German-bred dog. But for a gentle, family dog, look for an American Boxer."

4. Tendency to Bark/Vocalize

Some dogs are very excitable and will bark at the drop of a leaf outside. Other dogs rarely bark.

If constant yapping or houndlike baying bothers you, be sure to steer clear of the breeds and breed crosses that typically exhibit this behavior. Of course, if you want a canine alarm system, by all means invest in a dog that will alert you to strange goings-on.

5. Size

One of the beauties of dogs is that they come in so many shapes and sizes. Every mix and each breed looks strikingly different. Some people naturally gravitate toward smaller dogs such as those in the toy or terrier group. Others, such as myself, adore large dogs. But before you make an adoption, there are some considerations you need to make.

First of all, there's the issue of lifespan. Many of the large and giant breeds have a very short lifespan, eight years being the average not the exception. Some pass away as young as six years old! Compare this to small breeds such as poodles and other toys - or diminutive mixes - that routinely live to be twelve years old before they even begin to show signs of age-related problems. If you buy a giant breed dog, are you and your family prepared to part with your dog after so few years? Granted, there's no guarantee that a small or medium dog would live any longer but the odds are definitely not in the favor of a large breed.

There are some more subtle differences between small and large dogs, too. For example, in a family in which there is a rather unsteady toddler careening about, a smaller dog runs the risk of being squished by the toddler. If the toddler does fall on the dog, the combination of fear and pain may cause even the most patient little dog to bite! A large dog, on the other hand, may not be worried about the toddler at all. A sudden tumble, though uncomfortable, is not life threatening for the large dog. Of course, the bigger the dog, the bigger the bite.

Small dogs may get underfoot causing falls; boisterous large dogs routinely tumble toddlers, young children and adults alike. Small dogs can't get to high places; large dogs can pretty much pick and choose what they want to eat off the counter. Clean up with a small dog is easier than with a large dog. Giant-sized equipment, dog supplies and medication doses are more expensive for the large dog than for the small dog. There's a lot to consider.

Be sure to give the size of your prospective dog some thought. It is true that small and medium-sized dogs fit in a much wider range of home life scenarios than large and giant breeds; however, if you love large dogs, you can generally adapt your lifestyle to fit.

6. Coat Care

As was discussed briefly in the previous chapter, some coat types are simply more high maintenance than others. Some dogs are shorthaired, but shed profusely (Dalmatians). Other breeds appear to have shorthaired coats, but really aren't shorthaired dogs. Dr. Marsha Wallace, (English Cocker Spaniel Rescue), says that it's not uncommon for people to think that the English Cocker Spaniel is a shorthaired dog. "People will go to a dog show and see the dogs groomed and they say, 'Oh, they don't have much hair.' That's because in the show ring, the dogs are trimmed down to the point where they almost look like setters. Their body coats are really tight and they just have this little fringe. But give them a several weeks without grooming and you've got a different story!"

So, if you are interested in a breed that needs to be brushed daily, have its ears cleaned (drop eared dogs are prone to infections - and drip water and food bits across the floor), or have its coat trimmed, pulled, shaved, or otherwise worked on - you will either need to learn the techniques yourself, or be willing to pay roughly $30 for regular grooming sessions with a professional. If not, you could have an ugly, matted mess on your hands, not to mention things like sores and other nasty skin and coat conditions. Also, dogs with medium to long coats are quite adept at hiding ticks and fleas. If you live in an area of the country where these pests are a year-round problem, you will need to look into some effective flea/tick products.

Shedding. It should be a four-letter word, shouldn't it? Keep in mind that all dogs shed; it is nature's way of replacing old hair with new hair. And if someone tells you their dog doesn't shed, they're crazy. However, some dogs lose hair at a faster rate than others. When the dog has long hair, these lost hairs show up more easily in your house and clog up the vacuum cleaner.

Then there are seasonal coats and spring sheddings. With breeds that develop thick, luxurious winter coats, you can expect them to "shed" into a lighter coat in the spring and then there is hair everywhere. Oh yes, and if you think that a white dog is going to sleep on the white couch and his hairs won't show, forget it. Light colored dogs gravitate to darkly upholstered furniture and dark dogs seek out white furniture. It's kind of an unspoken canine law.

Then there are dogs with oily coats. Hunting dogs that are bred to hurl themselves into cold water and retrieve ducks and other dead waterfowl are going to have more oil in their coats than other dogs. When this coat is wet, it smells. When the dog hasn't been bathed in a while, it smells.

Keep in mind that you cannot continually bathe a dog to rid it of its oily coat without damaging its skin.

Of course, if you decide to skirt the whole issue of coats and care, you could buy a dog with no hair, (a Hairless Chihuahua comes to mind). You would alleviate the shedding, grooming and oily, wet coat problems, but could have to deal with dry skin and sunburns. It's always something, isn't it?

7. Temperament

By nature, most dogs are very devoted, loving animals, otherwise we would never have them in our homes! However, each breed has its little quirks, and it is best to know about them in advance. Even if you are buying a mixed breed, it is extremely important to understand the quirks of the breeds involved in your dog. When buying an adult dog, you are actually in a better position to judge the dog's temperament than with a puppy, but there are still several issues to look at.

Aggression

Aggression falls into several different categories. There are those dogs that are aggressive toward other canines and tend to bite. There are aggressive dogs that will bite people. There are dogs that will aggressively try to control their situation or "ranking" within the "pack" which includes their "human pack" and your small children. Some dogs will defend their home and family and are considered "territorially" aggressive. "Fear" aggression stems from the dog's response (biting) to fright. "Predatory" aggression is the most unstable in which the dog seeks out victims as a predator.

Though some forms of aggression, the most violent and unpredictable types, are now thought to stem from a chemical imbalance in the dog's brain, most other forms of aggression are believed to be a result of the dog's socialization (or lack thereof) as a puppy.

There are some breeds (and mixes of those breeds) that seem to have a history of more problems with biting and attacks. In general, breeds that are meant to guard or perform police work arebred to be confident. They are not afraid to protect your home, attack an intruder, and/or attack a person on command and they must be trained to defer to you, the owner, in their decision- making. An intelligent, well-bred, trained working dog can make an outstanding pet. On the other hand, an ill-bred, fearful, unsocialized Doberman, Rottweiler or German Shepherd Dog is extremely dangerous.

Breeds or mixes of breeds that were originally bred to dog fight or bait bulls may also be moreprone to get into trouble with aggression. Pit bulls are responsible for more dog related deaths than any other breed. (Runners-up were German Shepherds, Huskies, Malamutes, Dobermansand Rotties.)

Barbara McNinch, a professional trainer and Rottweiler owner, strongly recommends that anyone interested in adopted a working dog

(Doberman, Rottie, German Shepherd Dog, etc.) should avoid choosing a dog from a shelter. "I would definitely go with an organization that knows the breed very well and does extensive temperament evaluations. Breeders and breed rescues are great because these people will know much more about the dog's history and will have had the time to know the dog. In addition, they are experienced in placing this breed in a variety of homes." McNinch adds that if you must go to a shelter to choose this type of breed or a cross thereof, "You definitely want to take a pro with you to help in your decision. A veterinarian, a professional trainer, a breeder or a breed rescue person are all good choices." And if you have small children? "You should definitely think twice about adopting an adult. If the dog has not been exposed to children, it may not like children. That's a dangerous situation. Even by mistake, dogs such as these could hurt a child with its sheer size and strength. As a parent, you could never leave the two alone."

In a nutshell, if you have any misgivings with the dog, don't adopt it. There are enough beautifully tempered dogs in the world; why waste your time with a delinquent? Simply said: Don't buy or tolerate any inexcusable forms of aggression.

Submissiveness

Families with little children would most always be better off purchasing a submissive dog, one that is lower on the "totem pole," than a more dominant dog. A submissive dog will not try to boss you or your children around and will readily assume the bottom rank with no trouble.

Submissive dogs are not to be confused with fearful dogs as the former are generally very outgoing and friendly. If you're not familiar with the "sign" language of a submissive dog (the aversion of eye contact, turn of the head, dip of a shoulder, rolling over onto the back, even "smiling"), or if you might not be able to tell the difference between submissiveness and fright (tail between the legs, ears flat against the head, shaking, backing up, etc.), make sure you are working with someone who does (i.e., take a pro with you to the shelter).

8. Congenital diseases

Most breeds have certain diseases that crop up from time to time that are more prevalent than others. Breeders know what these diseases are and do their very best to breed out what they can.

Puppy mills and backyard breeders as a rule are not really concerned if they perpetuate these diseases and simply breed whatever dog is in season to an available male of the same breed. Mixed breeds, of course, are totally random joinings. Therein, lies the problem. Adult dogs that come from these less than desirable backgrounds may run a greater risk of inheriting something disagreeable.

However, take heart! With an adult dog, many of the hereditary diseases can be picked up on an x-ray or with a thorough veterinarian's examination. (Unlike a puppy which is a total "unknown.") Be aware of the various inflictions that could affect your breed of dog, or your mix of breeds, and how you can check for them. For example, Boxers are prone to heart disease. German Shepherds, Labrador Retrievers, Golden Retrievers and many other breeds may have difficulties with hip dysplasia. Dalmatians and Collies often go blind. St. Bernard's may be epileptic. Very large breeds like Great Danes are more susceptible to bloat. English Cocker Spaniels can develop "cherry eye." Protect yourself with as much knowledge as possible.

9. Destructiveness

Some breeds seem to get bored more easily than others. Unfortunately, a dog's response to boredom is usually some sort of destructive behavior. Will you need to crate the dog when you are out of the house? If you plan to keep your dog inside all of the time, and crating is not an option for you during the times you are not home, ask yourself this: Will it bother you if your newly adopted male Boxer rips down the blinds, curtains and shades while you are off running a few errands? (True story.) Would it upset you tremendously if your sweet little, couch potato Whippet decides there is something inside the cushion of your favorite couch and it is her mission to find it? (One of mine.) Aha, you say, but I plan to let the dog play in the yard when I step out to run errands! If you have a beautiful garden, will you get bent out of shape if your GSP carefully digs up every bulb you just planted and eats them? What if the breed you are interested in tends to jump? Labrador Retrievers, German Shepherd Dogs and others are notorious for scaling seemingly impassible fences. Are you prepared to make alterations to your yard, such as an inward sloping fence to keep your dog contained?

The key to minimizing destruction is to know what your breed (or mix of breeds) is likely to do and then take preventive measures. There is really nothing that a little time, ingenuity and love cannot overcome.

10. Male vs. Female

In some breeds, there really is not much difference in temperaments between the sexes. In others, there is. For example, track Greyhounds are very sweet, gentle and loveable as a whole. The males tend to be a little more happy-go-lucky and do not mind a little "rough" play from your children. (Hey, this is just another playmate!) The males also take corrections well, sometimes listening to you and sometimes not, but always forgiving you immediately for whatever it was you felt you had to scold them about. The females on the other hand take corrections very personally and may mope on a distant couch until you reassure them that you still love them. The girls invariably try to boss the boys around (we're talking dogs here), and the boys usually ignore them.

Whatever breed or mix of breeds you are interested in, be sure to ask if there is a temperament difference between sexes, particularly if you have children. Keep in mind, too, that even though some breeds may be known for their gentle dispositions this is no guarantee that every dog within that breed will be nice. Puppy mills and careless backyard breeders have a nasty way of developing or perpetuating bad temperaments. Just be careful. Also, "intact" males may be quite difficult to handle. Likewise, a female in season is no joy to have around the house. Unless you are planning to show or otherwise compete with your dog, it would be a good idea to have your dog neutered or spayed.

11. Trainability

Many adult dogs are surrendered because they have become too unruly for their owners or aren't housebroken. These dogs present a unique problem: You have a fully-grown, mature dog that still behaves like a puppy and has no manners. If you are experienced in obedience training and have housebroken countless other dogs, you know what you can handle and how much time you will have to put into the new dog's training. However, if you are a novice dog owner, be sure to understand what you are getting into.

If you are considering adopting a purebred, ask how easy this breed is to train. If the dog is small and is naturally an "obedient" sort, manners may not be a big issue except in the area of housebreaking. Fortunately, an adult dog has more control over its bodily functions than a puppy and should not have as many accidents. If the dog is large and exuberant, be sure you are capable of teaching the dog obedience and that you can enroll in a class immediately.

12. Indoor or outdoor?

"I don't like people to think that they're going to get a dog and then throw it out in the backyard all day," says Hendrickson (National Boxer Rescue). "I think it needs to be part of the family.

The general rule in my house is that if the air conditioning comes on, my dogs are in the house the majority of the time." Boxers are a brachycephalic breed which means their noses are so short that they cannot properly cool the air off that they inhale. As a result, Boxers and breeds like them have difficulties dealing with warm conditions. Hendrickson adds, "And when the heat's on and it's too cold for them to be out, they're inside. But they're still running around playing, getting exercise."

The ideal situation for a companion dog might be to give the dog the choice as to where it would like to be, letting it come in and out of the house at its leisure. However, for the safety of the dog and the sanity of the family, this is not always possible. Most dog people like to see a canine treated as a true member of the family. This does not mean you have to let the dog sleep in your bed, but the dog will be happiest if it can sleep in the house with its family and have regular human interaction. And always, always make sure the dog is comfortable.

How to find good information

Your level of "dog smarts" is critical to the success of selecting the perfect preowned dog and keeping your new canine happy. Even if you've owned a dog before, try to gain as much information as possible about dog breeds and dog behavior before signing for your adoption.

You'll find there's probably at least one or two things you didn't know or a few things you hadn't thought about. It is much better to make these discoveries before you bring home the dog! Here are a few places to begin your studies.

The Library

This is a good place to start. There are a lot of books on the market that offer tremendous information on dog behavior, training, specific breed information, and overall breed comparisons. Keep in mind that some books are better than others, while some are totally off the mark. (National Dalmatian Rescue warns of any books that suggest Dals make good pets for young children.) How do you find the best books? For recommendations, veterinarians are always good starting points as are local breed clubs, the national breed club secretary, or a well- respected, reputable breeder. (See Appendix A: National Breed Clubs and Breed Rescue.)

Much information can also be gleaned from such publications as AKC Gazette, Dog Fancy and Dog World. Behavior, nutrition and care are common topics. Also, most dog magazines run a monthly feature on a dog breed. Your librarian can help you locate the issue that highlights articles in which you are interested. If the library does not have a copy, you can usually write or call the circulation department of the magazine and order a copy of the particular issue you want.

Additionally, the new 1997 edition of Project BREED is extremely informative. (Old issues are good, too.) In the volume, there are one-page profiles for more than 150 breeds. What makes these descriptions so helpful is that they are written by the people who rescue that breed. "These people know why the dogs aren't working out and are being returned," says Lori Levin, president of Project Breed, Inc. "Unlike some breeders who would really like to sell you the dog and are perhaps blind to some of the breed's faults, the rescue people are a bit more realistic." In addition to breed profiles, the book also provides a listing of rescue contacts throughout the United States. If your library does not carry a copy of this volume, you can write for ordering information: Project BREED, Inc., P.O. Box 15888, Chevy Chase, Maryland 20825-5888.

Internet
You will be amazed at the wealth of information that can be found with a keystroke or two. A good place to begin researching AKC-registered breeds is with the AKC's website: http://www.AKC.org. Non-AKC registered breeds can usually be found by entering the breed's name in the search mode. There are also a plethora of sites with information on dog behavior and training. Since sites change virtually daily, the best way to get an updated listing is to run a search and then begin exploring. Or, get onto an online forum for dogs (such as CompuServe's) and post a message asking other members where their favorite places to go are.

Videos
Many of the more popular breeds now have videos. You can usually find these in pet stores or can order directly from various pet supply catalogs. The AKC also has a list of breed videos available.

A good video to watch if you have children, is Cats, Dogs and Kids: Learning to be Safe with Animals. The video is written by one of the country's foremost animal behaviorists, Wayne Hunthausen, D.V.M. Written specifically for children aged four to ten, it's a great flick to watch with your children. The video shows young people how to approach and handle pets safely and how to avoid actions that could lead to a sudden bite or nip. If you can't find this tape in your local pet stores, it can be ordered by calling: 1-800-784-0979 or writing: Pet love Partnership, LP, Suite 200, One East Delaware Place, Chicago, IL 60611; $19.95 plus $3.95 postage and handling.

National breed club publications

If you are interested in a particular breed, call the secretary of the national breed club and ask if they can send you some literature on the breed. This is good information written by the people who know. (And it's usually free.) The secretary can also tell you what books and videos are on their recommended reading list. (See Appendix A: National Breed Clubs & Breed Rescue.)

Local breed clubs

These clubs are a good source for breed information and information on reputable breeders in the area. To find a local breed club, look in the Yellow Pages under "kennel clubs" or call the national parent breed club secretary (Appendix A) and ask for the address and phone number of a local club in your area.

Reputable breeders

A reputable breeder will be happy to tell you all about his or her breed - its strong points and its pitfalls. They may even encourage you to come over and visit with their dogs. If you are offered this opportunity, go! There is no better way to learn about a breed than to sit down with the dogs and a breeder for an hour or so. If you have children, see how the dogs react to the kids and vice versa.

Dog shows

There's a time to talk to owners and a time not to talk to owners. If a show dog owner is standing by the ring, biting her nails and staring intensely at the judge as he goes over a dog, it would probably be best to leave that person alone, for the moment. Other owners don't get quite as wrapped up in show ring "goings on" and will warmly ask you to pull up a lawn chair next to theirs and proceed to talk your ears off. Other good places to talk to owners about their dogs are back in the grooming area or in the "sea of RVs." While waiting for show time, most owners are happy to answer your questions.

An advantage of going to a dog show is that you can see many different breeds and talk to lots of different people all in the same day. The only travel involved is moving from ring to ring. In addition, many dog clubs also set up information booths on their breed, and often on their rescueprograms, at dog shows. One more reason you should go!

Purebred rescue organizations

Almost every national breed club has established some sort of national network for rescue.

Rescue coordinators know their breed well. They are many times reputable breeders themselves.

Rescue organizations can tell you why their breed sometimes fails to flourish in a home and why.

They will be blunt about the breed's shortcomings. You can ask as many questions as you like and if they don't have the answer, they will know someone who does. They will not try to sell you a dog. If you would like to meet some adult rescue dogs, ask. There's no better way to learn about the breed. To find the rescue contact for the breed in which you are interested, see Appendix A: National Breed Clubs and Breed Rescue or Appendix B: Sources for Retired Track Greyhounds.

Veterinarians

If you have a veterinarian or know of one, he or she is an extremely valuable source for all kinds of information regarding dog behavior, illnesses, diseases, breed information, and even reputable sources for healthy, adult dogs.

Pet Fairs

An increasing number of pet stores are providing space for nonprofit placement organizations to "set up" right in the store. Weekends are usually times when these pet fairs are held and can be a great way to meet a certain breed or breeds and talk to some very knowledgeable people. To find out if a pet store in your holds regular pet fairs, simply call the stores in your area and ask if they hold pet fairs. If the store does, be sure to ask what groups are represented and when they are scheduled in the upcoming month.

CHAPTER 4
Breeders: Reputable and Not-So-Reputable

A reputable breeder is an outstanding source for adult dogs that is often overlooked. When we think of breeders, we mostly think of puppies. However, breeders will often have unadvertised dogs that are for sale or placement as well.

There are many reasons breeders may have an adult dog on hand. Sometimes breeders will have a retired show dog that, even though it is a champion, the breeder doesn't feel the dog is suitable for breeding. Breeders that specialize in field trial work may have hunting dogs that for one reason or another never really worked out in the field. Other times, a breeder may have sold a puppy years ago, only to have it returned as an adult because the original owners divorced, died or otherwise were unable to care for the dog. In addition, many breeders are active in breed rescue and from time to time will provide a foster home for a dog and assist with its placement.

One of the benefits of going to a reputable breeder is that you will receive a wonderful adult dog, one that is most likely well-bred, has had some training, and is well socialized. Another important advantage is that a breeder knows his or her breed and is very savvy when it comes to finding the right dog for the right home. And finally, you will have befriended a very knowledgeable dog person who can help you in all aspects of dog ownership, from finding a good veterinarian to advising on how to handle any behavior or health problems.

Of course, not all breeders are reputable. Breeders generally fall into one of several categories: Reputable, not-so-reputable, ignorant (backyard breeders), and unscrupulous (puppy mills). The quality of the dog and honesty of the breeder is naturally highest with a reputable breeder. After that, everything goes downhill at a fairly rapid rate. So, how can you tell with whom you are dealing?

Unscrupulous Breeders

Let's start with the worst first. There are people in this world that will do anything for a buck.

AKC-registered dogs are highly regarded in the United States and puppy millers have cashed in on this popularity. Puppy millers raise dogs as a commodity. They breed willy-nilly with no regard for health, temperament or conformation. Puppy millers produce as many pups as they can at the lowest cost possible which translates into a lot of poorly-bred dogs that are kept in miserable conditions and lack any socialization. An adult dog that is bought from a puppy mill may or may not be salvageable.

Tracy Hendrickson (National Boxer Rescue) recently went undercover to a dog auction and wound up rescuing several boxer females that had been used for years as breeding bitches. Hendrickson relates that the experience in attempting to socialize these poor canines was a horrendous ordeal - one that she might not go through again.

Ignorant Breeders

The people that fall into this category are one of the following: 1) Breeders who raise puppies solely for money but do it on a smaller scale than puppy mills, 2) people who decide to breed their dog to the neighbor's dog so they can have another dog just like the first one (plus ten other puppies that look just like her and have no homes), or 3) the parents who breed the family dog so the children can see the "miracle of birth." None of these individuals knows much about dogs - if anything. In addition, their actions contribute to the large number of unwanted dogs in ourcountry. The quality of dogs is generally poor. The dogs may or may not be treated well. The good news is that this class of breeders doesn't often have adults for sale - because they will never take back their puppies if things don't work out. (Occasionally you may find a "used" breeding bitch that can no longer breed.) As with the puppy mill breeding stock, this kind of dog could come with a lot of problems and is not recommended for inexperienced or novice dog owners.

Not-So-Reputable Breeders

Many breeders fall into this category--even those with multiple champions and legendary kennel names. What separates these breeders from their reputable counterparts are several subtle issues.

One, is that the not-so-reputable breeder may not be totally honest with a prospective buyer. This could include anything from "fudging" on the facts about the breed (i.e., Old Englishes don't shed, my St. Bernards have dry mouths, Jack Russells are very placid dogs, etc.) to outright lying about the dog's pedigree.

Carole DeAngelo, a marketing executive in West Virginia, recently bought what she thought was a purebred Cocker Spaniel from (what she thought) was a reputable breeder. When she picked out the pup, the breeder introduced her to the pup's mother (a buff) and told her the father was a black and white. DeAngelo was told that the pup had papers, but gee, he didn't know where they were so he would send them later. Totally in love with "Hardy," DeAngelo bought the pup and took her home. A few days later when she proudly carried her "AKC registered" pup into the vet's office for its first set of inoculations, she was floored with the vet's news. This puppy was by no means a purebred. Probably at least 25% Beagle. "The breeder denied everything," says DeAngelo. "He said there was no way she wasn't purebred. Now that she's older, there's no question that she's part Beagle." This is a perfect example of breeder dishonesty.

Another not-so-subtle difference between a disreputable breeder and one with a sterling reputation is that a less-than-desirable breeder will not take his or her dogs back. If you buy a dog only to realize that the dog has congestive heart failure, you're stuck. It's strictly buyer beware! You cannot return or exchange the dog for any reason.

Less-than-reputable breeders have also been known to make wild claims and unreal guarantees to the prospective buyer, a sort of hard-sell sales pitch. There may be little or no paperwork involved and the breeder may ask few questions of you or your home situation, displaying a lack of concern over the dog's future.

If you think you're dealing with a shady character, then you probably are. You'll be better off in the long run trying to steer away from breeders such as this and dealing only with reputable breeders.

Reputable Breeders

A reputable breeder's primary concern is not making money. A reputable breeder breeds for temperament, good health, and sound conformation. Their kennels are clean, and the dogs receive regular veterinary care. Good breeders are open about their pricing and will provide you with copies of any contracts that are involved. Additionally, they are almost always involved or supportive of breed rescue.

A reputable breeder is usually a member of the national breed club, perhaps active in a local club as well, and is an incredible source for breed information. He or she will know an awful lot about the breed's peculiarities, behaviors, feeding, grooming, effective training methods and more.

They should welcome your questions and make you feel you can call on them in the future if you are having any problems, need some advice, or even a referral. Once you have purchased your dog, a reputable breeder will turn over the dog's registration papers in a timely manner, usually when you leave with the dog or after you've met any responsibilities such as spaying or neutering.

If you have problems with you new acquisition, "a reputable breeder will cheerfully offer assistance and answer any question you may have on any aspect of the dog you got from them," comments Catherine Romaine Brown, owner of Treetop Kennels (Jack Russell Terriers). "This open and helpful relationship will last the life of the dog. Good breeders enjoy updates on how you are doing with their dog."

Most importantly, reputable breeders stand by what they sell and will take any dog that they have sold or bred at any time for any reason.

How to Find a Reputable Breeder

One of the best places to begin your search for a reputable breeder is with the national rescue chairperson for the breed. Why rescue? Because these people know which breeders take back their dogs and which don't. They know who is committed to breeding out congenital diseases and who isn't. They know. Call the breed rescue chairman and ask them for suggestions in your area. They will be more than happy to give you a referral. If the breed is registered with the AKC, you can tap into the AKC's list of national chairs for each of the breeds' rescue programs. Call the AKC for an updated list, because the names and numbers change periodically. If the breed you are interested in is not AKC registered, check for a listing in the Project BREED book or look through the breed advertisements in such publications as Dog World and Dog Fancy. Many times rare breeds will list their club or rescue network in these pages.

Another great place to find reputable breeders is with "Breeder Referral Contact" from the breed you are interested in. All AKC registered breeds have a designated person for the explicit purpose of helping people find reputable breeders. Be sure to ask this person what their requirements are for a breeder to be listed. If all a breeder has to do is pay a fee to be listed, this is NOT a list of reputable breeders. You might also try calling the secretary of the breed club.

Again, if the breed is AKC-registered, you can get this information from the AKC. The breed club secretary is sure to be able to give you some names and numbers in your area to get you started. If the breed is not recognized by the AKC, you can probably find the club secretary through the classified advertising in the dog magazines listed above.

How to Choose an Adult Dog From a Breeder
The Initial Phone Call & Telephone Interview

So you've been asking around and have finally found a breeder that thinks they might have a dog available. What do you do now? First of all, when you call the breeder be sure to introduce yourself, explain that you are looking to buy an adult dog (for a pet, as a hunting companion, for performance events, etc.), you heard that they might have one you would be interested in, and that so-and-so referred you. Don't forget to tell the breeder who told you to call! This helps solve the mystery as to how you got their phone number!

After you've completed this introduction, be prepared to be interviewed over the telephone by the breeder. He or she will want to know why you are interested in buying an adult dog, why you want this particular breed, what you are looking for in a dog, what your family life is like, how you plan to care for your dog while at work, whether the dog will be an inside or an outside dog, what your lifetime experience has been with dogs, what your experience has been with this particular breed, if you have any small children, if you have any other pets, if you have a fenced backyard, and many other questions.

"I screen every home very carefully," says Brown. "[Jack Russell Terriers] must have a fenced yard and an owner who knows what the dog is all about. Without knowledge, the JRT is a bit of a loaded gun."

Don't be offended by this interrogation! Breeders (the reputable ones) are very particular about where their dogs go, even their pet quality canines. If you have done your homework on the breed, and are very open and genuine with the breeder, he or she will warm up quickly to you.

A word of warning: Your first question to the breeder should not be, "How much are you charging for this dog?" It is appropriate, however, to find out sometime during the phone conversation if the dog is within your price range. You just don't want the breeder to think that price is the only reason you are interested in an adult dog! Save this question for the end of the conversation and perhaps rephrase it to: "Do you have an idea as to about how much you might want for (Fill in dog's name here)?" If the breeder is a little vague with his or her answer, don't worry too much. They may not have considered selling this dog. Or perhaps the breeder is waiting to meet you and your family first.

The Kennel Visit

If you pass muster on this initial phone conversation, then the breeder will generally invite you over to their home to show you the adult dog. Breeders are generally quite proud of their kennels and should give you a quick tour or bring the dogs inside their home to introduce to you. On this visit, it is your turn to ask all the questions. If you have concerns regarding care, temperament, conformation, or anything else you can think of - ask! There is no such thing as a stupid question and the breeder would much rather you had the right information than be harboring a misconception.

When the dog is in the kennel, observe how it interacts with its kennel mates. Is it a domineering sort? Or, does it seem to be everyone's playmate? If the new dog is not going to be an "only" dog, it is particularly important that it is well socialized with other canines.

When it's time for you to meet the dog, you should be able to have some one-on-one time with the dog away from distractions. Observe the dog's behavior very carefully. Does it come to greet you? Does it enjoy being petted? Hugged? Can you play with it? Feed it cookies? Take objects out of its mouth? How does the breeder interact with the dog? Does he or she have to use a firm voice?

If you have children, take them with you. Explain to them that you are just going to look, not to buy. In fact, take your whole family. See how the dog interacts with your family members. Is it playful? Placid? Does it show any signs of dominance or aggression toward your children? Have the breeder show your children how to pet the dog, brush the dog and otherwise handle the dog. Let him or her also tell your children what not to do with the dog. Even if they know this, it helps to have a stranger reinforce it.

If the breeder shows any concerns or hesitations about letting you buy the dog, talk to him or her openly about these concerns. The breeder may have picked up on some subtle nonverbal signals from the dog that might indicate trouble. When an individual specializes in one particular breed, as a breeder does, they are very adept at picking up on subtleties that even other dog people may not catch. Trust them. If for any reason they feel the match is not one made in heaven, go with their opinion.

Similarly, if for any reason you are hesitant about the dog, wait. Don't make an impulsive decision just because you've got two little children be ging to take Rupert home. Be sure to discuss your hesitation with the breeder. Sometimes it may be a well-founded concern and other times not. For instance, some breeds "smile." The dogs will wrinkle their noses up and expose all of their teeth. For those who have never seen a dog do this, it can be quite frightening.

However, it truly is a friendly, submissive gesture and is quite different than a snarl in which the teeth are also exposed - but not in the same way.

The Home Visit

Some breeders opt to visit with you at your home before they will sell or place a dog. This gives the breeder an opportunity to see if you've really been telling the truth about your living arrangements. If the breeder brings a dog with him or her, it also gives the breeder an opportunity to see how the breed will fit into your lifestyle.

The Purchase

Let's say you've passed muster with the breeder, you and your family have really hit it off with the dog as well as the breeder, and you've agreed to buy or adopt the dog. Your work is only half finished. Any breeder that is worth his or her salt will now inundate you with paperwork and legalese. Don't be intimidated! It's just another guarantee that the dog receives a good and final home.

As a buyer or adopter, you should receive the following items:

> **Pedigree:** If the dog was bred by the breeder, he or she should be able to provide you with a copy of the dog's three generation pedigree. The pedigree will show all of your dog's immediate ancestors along with their AKC titles and various certificates of health. The pedigree may be a copy filled in by the breeder (unofficial) or one provided by the AKC (official).
>
> Non-AKC breeds also have pedigrees. For example, breeders of registered Jack Russell Terriers should provide new owners with a signed, four (or more) generation pedigree and a signed stud service certificate (no mystery daddies, here!).
>
> **Registration papers:** These papers are from the AKC and show the transfer of ownership of the dog from the day it was

born. When you buy the dog, the breeder will show you where you have to sign the papers. The papers are then sent back to the AKC to register the transfer of ownership.

You will receive copies in the mail.

Limited Registration: If the dog was originally sold as a pet quality dog, the breeder may have given the original owner limited registration on the dog. This means that the dog is registered with the AKC, but that it is spayed or neutered and is limited to participating only in certain events.

Indefinite Listing Privilege (ILP) - If the dog you are buying is a purebred but has no papers (perhaps it is a dog that the breeder rescued from another source), you can still compete in many of the AKC's performance events and obedience by getting an ILP. The process for this involves sending photographs of the dog along with a completed application to the AKC along with a minimal fee.

Health Certifications - When a dog is radiologically proven to have sound hips (x-rayed for hip dysplasia and found to be clear of disease), the dog may be issued a number from the Orthopedic Foundation for Animals (OFA). Elbow joints may also be certified through the OFA. Labrador Retrievers may have a Wind-Morgan number as well, certifying that their elbows, shoulders, hips and hocks are normal. There are also certifications for inheritable eye diseases (Canine Eye Registration Foundation) and tests for hypothyroidism. The breeder can point out the acronyms on the dog's pedigree and explain what the test is for and the value of having this testing completed.

Breed Information - Owning a dog is a continual learning process. There's always something new to learn. The breeder will probably give you some pamphlets or handouts on the breed which should be very helpful. He or she may also give you a recommended reading list of personal favorites as far as books on the breed, training and dog behavior.

A Return Guarantee - Among your stack of information from the breeder, you should receive a guarantee in writing that he or she will take back the dog if for any reason you are dissatisfied or the match doesn't work for one reason or another. Reputable breeders stand behind what they sell and are proud of the dogs. Most likely this will be one of the first documents you will receive.

Sales Contract - This contract varies from breeder to breeder but will generally give the vitals on the dog, a registration number, any certification numbers, and an abbreviated pedigree. It may also include a requirement that you agree to take good care of the dog. If you are found to be lax in this requirement, the breeder reserves the right to take the dog back. The return guarantee may also be included in this document as well as the liability waiver.

Sales Receipt - You will probably only receive a sales receipt if you pay cash for your dog.

Otherwise, your canceled check will usually serve as your receipt. If the breeder takes MasterCard or Visa, you probably aren't doing business with a reputable person who breeds selectively.

Spay/Neuter Contract - If the dog is not already spayed or neutered, the breeder may have you sign a spay/neuter contract. By signing this contract, you are agreeing to have your dog spayed or neutered within a specified time frame. You will also be required to provide the breeder with proof from the veterinarian that the services were performed and to the correct dog. If you do not fulfill your end of the contract and neglect to have your dog altered, the breeder can take the dog back. The reason for the spay/neuter contract is a sound one: Once the surgery is performed, the dog cannot be bred. Requiring a spay/neuter helps to deter profit-seekers from buying the dog for breeding stock. It also is healthier for your dog and prevents the inconvenience often incurred with intact or fertile dogs. Additionally, it prevents bringing any more unwanted dogs into the world.

AKC Registration Withholding Agreement - This is another means of guaranteeing that the buyer spays or neuters the dog. If the owner doesn't spay or neuter, he or she will not receive the dog's papers, insuring that any puppies that might result from this dog are not AKC registerable.

Liability Waiver - You may have to sign a waiver of liability. This may be a separate piece of paper or included in the sales contract. Regardless of its location, the waiver releases the breeder from any liability or responsibility for any accident, damage or injury resulting from the sale of the dog.

Co-Ownership - The breeder may choose to retain partial ownership of the dog so that co-owner can never sell, give away or turn the dog over to the pound without consulting the breeder first.

This makes sense in that the breeder can keep a watchful eye on the health and welfare of his or her dog. If the dog is being abused or mistreated in any other way, the breeder has more legal leverage to take the dog back.

Before You Bring Your Dog Home

It is critical that before you go to the breeder to pick up your dog, or the breeder is scheduled to deliver the dog to you, you have everything set up in your home for your new dog. Have the breeder tell you what type and size of collar the dog needs. Purchase a leash, brush, dog bed, maybe a few toys and a chew. The dog will need its own food and water bowls (not plastic which can cause gingivitis). Ask the breeder what type of food the dog is currently eating and buy a sufficient supply of it. An abrupt change in diet can cause incredible cases of diarrhea! Find out what size crate the dog will need to be very comfortable and what type of crate the dog is used to.

Some dogs prefer the closed-in den varieties, whereas, others enjoy the open, mesh type.

And, don't forget! Even if your dog is obedience trained, enroll in a class and train yourself--or help the dog brush up on his commands. A well-trained dog is a joy to have around the house.

Also, remember that if you ever have any questions, never hesitate to call the breeder. He or she would much rather help you nip a difficulty in the bud than let the problem progress to an escalated stage. Oh yes, and enjoy!

CHAPTER 5

Breed Rescue

There are some misconceptions about purebreds that need to be rectified. First of all, many people think purebreds don't need rescuing because they rarely end up in shelters. Not so.

According to a spokesperson from the Humane Society of the United States, "Around 25 percent of the dogs in shelters are purebreds. Depending on the part of the country, it can be as high as 50 percent."

The second rumor that needs to be put to rest is that if a purebred is given up, it must be there because it has a really serious problem. This simply isn't true. If a purebred becomes inconvenient or an owner isn't willing to spend a little time and effort to work a dog through a behavior problem (such as jumping up on visitors), the dog that once had a price tag of $700 to $1,000 will quickly find its way to the shelter. Unfortunately, many people who visit shelters don't realize this fact, increasing the chances of the purebred being euthanized.

Realizing that far too many good purebred dogs were being turned into shelters and that the chances of adoption for these purebreds were actually less than that of a mixed-breed, the idea for breed rescue was born.

Twenty years ago, there were only a few individuals rescuing a handful of breeds. Today, that number has grown to include hundreds of rescue organizations across the country, representing nearly every AKC-registered breed. There are local, regional and national breed rescue organizations, many of which have formed a national network of rescuers that is supported by the national breed club. In other instances, several local rescue groups have joined efforts and formed multi-breed or all-breed rescue organizations.

The strides these groups have made in the past two decades are impressive. Most breed rescue workers are heavily involved in the breed either through showing, obedience or performance events. Their level of breed knowledge is astounding. The organization and services these rescuers provide are unparalleled. And best of all? One hundred percent of placeable dogs that enter the breed rescue system find homes. Those that are ill-tempered or in the last stages of a terminal condition (e.g., advanced heartworm) and cannot be placed in a home are painlessly euthanized by injection with a veterinarian and lovingly cradled by a rescue worker.

Of course, there's a flip side to breed rescue that isn't so pretty. Some so-called rescues are actually fronts or brokers for puppy mills, collecting and selling breeding stock. Others are "collectors" of animals, keeping entirely too many animals in cramped, deplorable and filthy conditions. This is animal abuse, not rescue.

How do you know if you've found a reputable breed rescue? When you visit the rescuer's home, you should know pretty quickly. If the rescue worker won't let you visit, this should be a red flag warning! First of all, the living quarters of the dogs, the rescue worker's home and/or kennel, should be clean and the exercise areas well "picked up." There shouldn't be any dogs tied up in the yard or in crates "out back" in the barn. The rescuer's personal dogs should be healthy, happy and with no signs of being mistreated. In addition, the rescue worker should be polite, professional and willing to freely share breed information, both pros and cons, with you.

Anything less, and you're not dealing with a reputable rescue worker.

How to Find a Breed Rescue

One of the simplest ways to find a good breed rescue is to call the AKC and ask for the address and phone number of the current national rescue chairperson for the breed in which you are interested. This person will be able to tell you all about the breed club's rescue program and give you the name of the person who is in charge of your area or region. (See Appendix A: Breed Clubs and Rescues.)

If you call the AKC and they don't have a listing for a national rescue chairperson, don't fret!

Ask for the name and number of the breed secretary. He or she will probably know at least one person who is involved in rescue - which will get your toe in the door.

Another excellent source for finding breed rescues is the book, Project BREED (Breed Rescue Efforts and Education Directory). Check to see if your library or local humane society has a current copy. If not, a copy can be obtained by sending an SASE for current directory price and ordering information to: Project BREED, P.O. Box 15888, Chevy Chase, MD 20825-5888.

Project BREED is a "Yellow Pages" of breed rescue groups across the United States. Some groups are affiliated with the national breed clubs. Others are not. Lori Levin, president of Project BREED, Inc., cautions that any person who wants to list their rescue organization can do so. The only screenings the rescues receive is a telephone interview. Rescues are not inspected by Project BREED. In other words, proceed with your eyes open! Don't take anything for granted!

How Breed Rescues Operate

Breed rescues are generally affiliated, though not necessarily, with either a national breed club or a local/regional breed club. If the rescue organization is associated with a national breed club, it is most likely part of a large, national network of rescuers. If the breed rescue is affiliated with local breed club, it too could be part of a large national network or it could be a solo effort. Most breed rescue organizations concentrate on rescuing only one breed. Occasionally you might find a multi-breed or all-breed rescue in which several breed rescues have joined forces.

There are several ways in which purebred dogs find their way into the loving hands of a breed rescue worker. Many times, dog owners will hear of a local rescue group and will surrender their dogs directly to the rescue organization. Other times, the rescue worker will receive an anonymous call that one of their "breed" is loose and could they please come and pick it up? Shelters and pounds may call a breed rescue if they've received a purebred that they don't feel they can place. Other times, the rescue organization will regularly send "scouts" to shelters and pounds to see if there are any dogs there that they hadn't been told about.

And then there are instances in which a rescue worker receives a report that a dog is being severely mistreated and/or abused. In some cases, the worker will visit the home. If the conditions are deplorable and the dog is in serious trouble, the worker may offer to buy the dog from the owner. If the owner refuses to sell the dog, and the situation warrants it, the worker may call animal control and pick up the dog once it's at the shelter.

Once the breed rescue has the dog in its possession, the first thing the director will do is, if possible, get as much information as possible about the dog. If the dog is being surrendered, the rescue worker tries to find from the owner such things as: What the dog's home life was like; its daily routine; its likes, dislikes, and fears; behavior problems; training; exposure to children and what ages; shot records; health problems; how it behaves around other animals (cats and dogs); whether the dog is housebroken; spayed or neutered; if the dog is AKC registered; a general temperament description; and the reason for turning over the dog.

If the dog is being adopted out of the shelter, the rescue worker is unable to question the priorowner and must rely on the questionnaire that was filled out by the owner when the dog was dropped off. Unfortunately, many times owners don't take the time to fill out the form very thoroughly and leave most of it blank. Other times, the person will fill out the form in its entirety, but may "fudge" a bit with the facts (i.e., saying their dog is housebroken when it's really not or vice versa). And in unorganized shelters, it's not uncommon for shelter workers to be unable to find the dog's information. Of course, the dogs that were picked up as strays have no information sheet. In all of these cases, the rescue worker tries to talk with any shelter workers or volunteers that have come in contact with the dog and may have noticed an thing of interest.

Before the rescue person leaves the shelter, he or she signs the shelter's adoption papers, pays the adoption fee and then off they go. This is just the beginning!

Usually before the rescue worker takes the dog home, he or she will make a stop by the vet's office for a complete checkup and any necessary shots or medications. Once the dog is given a clean bill of health, the rescue worker will do one of two things: Either take the dog home or take the dog to a foster home.

Most larger rescue organizations have a network of people who are willing to take in one or two dogs at a time for periods of a week to a month or more. While the dog is living at the foster home, it is groomed, handled, medicated (if prescribed), and played with. During this time period, the dog is also carefully being evaluated by the foster "mom" or "dad." Foster parents look for such things as aggression, shyness, fearfulness, and toler- ance of children. In addition, many times foster parents will housebreak the dog and begin a little basic obedience work. By the time the dog is ready to leave the foster home, the rescue workers usually have a pretty good feel for what kind of canine they are dealing with, whether it likes children or not, if it's aggressive or timid, etc.

Once the dog is adopted out to a new owner, the rescue doesn't stop its efforts! Most breed rescues will follow-up with at least a phone call to make sure that everyone is doing well. Breed rescues are a terrific source of information, and many new owners find themselves calling rescue a number of times for things as simple as a referral to a veterinarian or as complex as solving a troublesome behavior.

If for any reason the adoption does not work out, the breed rescue will take back the dog. If the problem was with the dog (maybe it refused to coexist peacefully with the family cat), the rescue will usually try to give the family a replacement rescue dog.

"I had a dog come back recently that I had adopted out to a family two months ago," explains Tracy Hendrickson, national chairperson for Boxer Rescue. "He was a young dog, a gun shot wound dog, and turned out to be just too much for their kids. So I said, 'Bring it back. I've got another, older sedate dog that I'd like you to try.'" The family came, made the exchange and offered to pay Hendrickson another adoption fee. "I said, 'No, you've already paid your $95 to go to a dog's vet bills. There's no reason for you to pay it again. I just want to make sure you get the dog that you expect."

Of course, the terrific services that breed rescue offers all take an incredible investment of time and a substantial amount of money. First, there are costs incurred transporting the dog to the rescue worker's home. This might be as inexpensive as driving to a shelter only a few minutes away to potentially traveling to a location several hours away. Hendrickson reports having even flown in some dogs from out-of-state that couldn't be handled locally.

Secondly, if the dog is coming from a shelter, the rescue worker must pay the shelter's adoption fees in order to release the dog from the shelter - anywhere from $20 to $75. Many shelters charge substantially more in adoption fees for purebred dogs. Then, there's the immediate trip to the veterinarian. Depending on what the dog needs (i.e., vaccinations, worming, flea dip, spay/neuter, etc.), the fees can run anywhere from $50 to $150 or more. But wait, there's more! While the dog is at the foster home, there's food that needs to be bought and perhaps medicines to administer. Equipment such as crates, beds, collars, etc., are an up-front expense, but the equipment should last for several years.

As you can see, rescuing a dog is not cheap! It not only takes a dedicated network of volunteers and lots of love, but cold, hard cash as well. Some rescue organizations receive financial support from their national breed club; however, most must find funds on their own. In other words, fundraising is an important facet of rescue to keep the adoption costs to a minimum. Adoption fees usually range from $90 to $250, which is sometimes only a fraction of the costs involved when a dog requires extensive veterinary care. Some breed rescues don't even have an adoption fee, rather they ask that the adopting owner give a donation in an amount of his or her choosing (and as conscience dictates . . .).

What to Expect From a Breed Rescue

There are two things about breed rescue that consistently surprise most people. One is the amount of time involved in the rescue application process. A month, from beginning to end, is not unusual. The second aspect that throws many off is the co prehensive interviewing and background checking that is performed before a person is allowed to adopt a dog. One owner confessed that adopting her collie was "as hard as adopting a child!"

Please don't let these factors deter you from going through breed rescue! The rescuers have the best interest of the dog at heart and simply want to make sure that the dog is going to a good and final home. Of course, if you don't feel comfortable with the rescue person you are working with, by all means contact someone else. In every organization there are bound to be a few bad apples!

You should never have to deal with someone who isn't pleasant.

In addition, keep in mind that every rescue group - even within the same breed - handles their rescues a little differently. Some groups won't consider any applicant who doesn't have a fenced yard. Others feel that given the right owner in the right situation, a fenced yard is not a mandatory precondition to adoption. For example, for some dog breeds, the owner who takes his dog to work may be able to function very well without a fenced yard. Or the owner who has an in-home business and enjoys taking a break and walking her dog every four hours or so can also make a fenceless yard a doable proposition.

The Adoption Process From a Breed Rescue

The first step in adopting an adult dog from a breed rescue is to find a reputable breed rescue organization in your area that you feel comfortable working with. (See Appendix A: National Breed Clubs and Rescues.) Once you've located a group, give them a call. Many rescuers have full-time jobs (in addition to the full-time job of rescuing purebreds), so be patient if it takes a day or two before they return your call.

When you do talk to the rescue person, be prepared for a friendly, "sizing up" over the phone.

You'll probably be asked why you want to adopt a dog, how you found out about breed rescue, and what your experiences have been in the past with this breed and any other dogs.

This initial contact is also your chance to talk to the rescue worker about the breed and how they operate. If you're concerned about the breed's activity level, grooming requirements, potential congenital diseases, or anything else - ask! You will receive a very honest answer. Remember, the rescue workers aren't trying to sell dogs, they're trying to place formerly unwanted dogs.

They know better than anyone else why these dogs aren't working in homes! A good rescue worker should welcome your questions and freely share breed information with you.

After this phone conversation, you will most likely be mailed an application form to complete and return to the rescue organization.

The Application

Questions will vary, but in general you'll be asked to provide two sets of information. The first section is typically personal background information: Your address and phone number; your reason for wanting a rescued dog; if you have a fenced yard; if the yard is shaded; whether you intend to keep the dog indoors, outdoors, or both; if you have children, their ages and their experience with dogs or other pets; if you have any other dogs or pets currently in the home; and your own dog experience (number of dogs owned, when you owned them, how they died, etc.)

The second half of the application will ask you what you are looking for in your rescued dog, such as: Male or female; age range; AKC registered or not; color; and what you would like to be able to do with your dog (obedience, hunt, lure coursing, tracking, etc.).

There are no really right answers to this questionnaire, but there are some definite "no-no's." A dog that will be left outside at all times is not an acceptable situation nor is tying a dog to a stake in the backyard or crating a dog for 8 to10 hours at a time. Remember, though, when answering this questionnaire, you must be painfully honest. If you realize something in your situation is less than perfect but you are willing to come up with a viable alternative, let the rescue know this.

Your honesty and sincerity in answering these questions will pay back tenfold. Not only will the rescue worker gain a sense of trust in you, in addition, forthright answers will also help him or her eventually place the best dog possible with you for your situation.

The Interview

Once you've mailed in your application, you can expect a call back from someone from the breed rescue in a week or so. Don't be impatient if it takes awhile to receive an answer. As mentioned earlier, most rescue workers have other full-time jobs and rescue work can be extremely time consuming. It's perfectly O.K., though, to call the breed rescue and confirm that your application was received and if there's anything else you need to send.

When you do get a call back on your application, the interviewer will go over your questionnaire with you and perhaps ask some additional questions. Be sure to keep in mind that all of these questions are ultimately to find the rescued dog a good home. "These dogs have been through a lot," explains Emma Jean Stephenson, national rescue coordinator for the Dachshund Club of America. "A lot of Dachshunds come to me after living with someone for six or seven years. The owners drop them off because for one reason or another the dog is now inconvenient. All of a sudden the little dog is totally lost. Its whole world is falling apart. It's as if someone were to pick you up and drop you off a hundred miles away from home and tell you that you'll never see your relatives, family or friends again. They look at me with such a look in their eyes that I just feel so sorry for them." Stephenson adds, "So when I place a dog in a second home, I want to make sure it is a good home and a permanent home."

People that are turned down by breed rescue are usually those whose lifestyles or living arrangements don't meet the needs of the dog. "People get so upset when we turn them down because they live in an apartment," relates Catherine Romaine Brown, national humane officer of the Jack Russell Terrier Club of America "Russell Rescue" with a heavy sigh. "But a Jack Russell Terrier cannot take apartment life. They have an enormous activity level and require a lot of exercise, attention and a place to channel their mental activity. This dog is a country hunting dog and is not for cities. We've had dogs that have dug through walls and subflooring to get out of the house or to hunt rodents. Another person had to take a backhoe to dig their dog out of a drain pipe in their backyard. Jack Russells are a really tricky little dog to manage and they simply are not for everybody."

The Home Visit

If all goes well during the interview stage, many rescue groups schedule a home visit. This is exactly what it sounds like. A rescue worker comes to your home, sometimes with a dog, and visits you. By meeting you in person in your home, a good dog person can quickly ascertain whether or not you will make a good home for this breed. They will probably want to discuss with you the importance of training, vaccinations, proper care of dogs in general, and other such issues.

If the rescue worker brings a dog with him or her, this is also a great time for you to get to meet one of the breed. You will be able to see whether this breed will work out well in your home. People who like to put curios on their coffee tables may not have realized that a mid-sized dog's tail can knock everything off with just a properly placed wag or two. Or, that a Dachshund is athletic enough to get up on the dining room table via an end chair. Sometimes children react differently to dogs than their parents would expect. A big dog might be frightening. A little dog might seem like a toy (not good). Take advantage of this home visit and learn as much as you can about the breed, too.

Introduction to the Breed

If the rescue didn't require a home visit, they will probably ask you to come over to the rescue "center" (usually a breeder's home or kennels). "I call it a 'meet the Boxer' night," laughs Hendrickson. "I turn my crew out [eight Boxers] and let the people play tug of war and watch them run in the yard and then sit around in the living room and generally just get to know the breed. I really think there's no better way to understand a particular breed than to be surrounded by a roomful of them. You can really learn a lot in just an hour or so. I tell people if they have children, to bring them, too. It gives me an opportunity to see how the children react to the dogs and if they're going to treat dogs really well. I get a better feel for the best match for the entire family this way."

Depending on how the particular breed rescue works, you may even be able to meet the dog they have in mind for you. However, don't get your hopes up. Many times you will be put on a waiting list.

The Waiting List

Ah, the dreaded waiting list. I know what you're thinking: If there are so many dogs in desperate need of a home, why on earth would they put people on a waiting list? This tends to be particularly disturbing if you really, really want a dog and you know that the rescue has three or four dogs waiting for homes right now. Don't be upset. There are several reasons for a waiting list. One is to determine if you really are serious about owning a rescued dog or if it's just a passing fancy to "save" a dog. I know of at least one breed rescue that routinely makes people wait a

month before placing a dog with them. Not surprisingly, this wait weeds out a lot of people who perhaps became interested in rescue only because of its heartstrings tugging "cause," not because they seriously wanted a dog, once they had considered everything.

The second, and most common, reason for a waiting list is simply to find the dog best suited to your situation. Sure, the rescue may have six dogs waiting for homes but they could all be the type of dog you're trying to avoid. Trust the rescue.

A third reason for the waiting list is that some breed rescues don't get many dogs in. Breeds that are not as popular do not have as great a problem with unwanted dogs. So, if you're dying to adopt an Irish Wolfhound, you may have to wait awhile before one needs rescuing. But don't worry. Irish Wolfhound rescue will gladly take your name.

Of course, there are some breed rescues that can't afford the luxury of a waiting list. In fact, they may have several dogs on hand with no adoption prospects in sight. There will be other times when the rescuer will happen to have a perfect match for you right then and there. Anything can really happen. What you will find in the way of waiting lists will many times vary with the area of the country, the rescue group themselves, and the breed involved. Just remember, if you are put on a waiting list, don't be offended! It's not because the rescuer didn't like the color of your hair or the shoes you wear. It's because they know what kind of dog (temperament, activity level, training, etc.) will do best in your home and they know that it's just a matter of time before that dog ends up at rescue. In other words, you'll end up with a much better match if you wait for the perfect paring than if you demand to be paired with whatever canine is on hand. Trust the rescuers. They are breed experts and will do the best job they can for you!

Also, another thought. Be flexible. If you've requested a yellow female lab not older than two and the Lab rescue calls up and says, "Hey, we've got this 3-year-old chocolate male we'd like you to take a look at . . ." - go take a look! The rescue wouldn't have called you if they didn't think the dog was perfectly suited for your needs. It's just that the sex and color may be a little different than you first thought you'd like. If you really can't be flexible, then do be prepared to wait. If your request is particularly hard to fill, for example a rare color, then you may have to wait a very long time before the dog of your dreams trots into your life.

Your New Dog

When the breed rescue calls and tells you that they have a dog they'd like you to come look at, it's O.K. to get excited, but don't let your hopes get too high. First of all, make sure to bring every family member with you to meet the dog. It is important that everyone in the family be as excited and dedicated to giving the new dog a good home as you are. It is equally important to see how the dog reacts to all members of the family. Listen carefully to what the breed rescue people tell you about the dog; they are a wealth of information. If the dog has been in a foster home for two weeks or more, the rescue group will know an awful lot about the dog. If the dog has only been fostered for a day or two, there may still be a lot to learn. However, this is where the beauty of dealing with breed rescue comes in.

Most people involved in purebred rescue are also experts in their particular breed. They're specialists, so to speak. They can pick up on subtle nonverbal behaviors that you, not having been "in the breed" for twenty years or more, might not pick up on or understand their possible implications.

Go with your own impressions of the dog, too. Is it love at first sight? Or are you more apprehensive? If you are unsure of the match, ask yourself, "Why?" Are you intimidated by the dog? Are members of your family uneasy? If so, it's not a good match. The dog will know it has the upper hand even if it isn't inclined to exert its power. Do you think the dog is too active?

Ask the rescue worker what he or she thinks. It could be the dog is just very excited to have visitors. If you have any concerns, now is the time to voice them and get answers.

Most likely you'll be like most dog people and the moment you lay eyes on the dog you'll realize you absolutely must have this dog even if it isn't exactly what you expected to see. Dogs of all shapes and sizes have a way of very quickly working their way into our hearts and permanently staying there. Once you've found the dog you want, there's still some paperwork to get through.

The Paperwork

If the rescue group adopted the dog out of a shelter, they should be able to provide you with those records which will many times include the information sheet the previous owner filled out, which may or may not be entirely factual. If the dog was surrendered to rescue, the prior owner(s) should have signed a paper acknowledging their willing surrender of the dog to rescue This paper prevents the former owner(s) from coming back later and attempting to take the dog away from its adopted owner. You may or may not be able to see this (there may be some confidentiality issues), but your rescue worker can confirm or deny that this procedure was done.

In addition, the rescue group should be able to provide you a copy of the dog's veterinary work- up, detailing what shots were given, what work-ups were performed, a general health summary and other pertinent information and observations. If the dog was not spayed or neutered, you will be required to sign a spay/neuter contract. Typically, this operation must be performed in a prescribed number of days. When you have the spay/neuter completed, you will need to provide the rescue with the veterinary records. Failure to have a dog spayed or neutered under a contract such as this may result in your forfeiture of the dog and the adoption fee. Don't be a bad toad; get it done! And promptly!

You'll also need to sign a contract. Again, every rescue has its own version, but the most typical contracts require the following:

1. **Transfer of ownership** - Most rescues require that if you are unable to keep your dog for any reason, you may not sell or give your dog away. It must be returned to the breed rescue. Other rescues will not give you "ownership" of the dog until you've gone through a trial period with the dog. Some rescues never transfer the ownership; in these instances, the dog is technically the property of the breed rescue and therefore can be reclaimed at any time for any reason (usually an unsatisfactory home).

2. **Care** - The contract may require the new owner to agree to maintaining a satisfactory level of care for the dog, including adequate food, water, veterinary care, etc. Of course, one would hope that the new owner would go far beyond what is "satisfactory," but in the rare cases when something does go awry this clause gives the rescue the authority it needs to reclaim the dog.

3. **Control** - The rescue may spell out their restrictions as far as requiring a fenced back yard or keeping the dog "under voice control or on lead at all times." Rescues aren't likely to take exception to adopters who break this rule. Accidents do

happen, dogs have been known to slip away from their owners, but if your adopted dog has to be re-rescued by its breed rescue, don't expect to get the dog back in the near future.

4. **Damages** - There should be a clause in the contract that the adopter agrees to hold harmless the breed rescue if the adopted dog causes any damage. For example, if you leave the dog loose in your house and you return home to find that it has chewed through the leg of your genuine, Marie Antoinette dining room table, you can't hold the breed rescue responsible for the cost of replacing the table leg.

5. **An "Everything Else, Too" Clause** - This is the clause that rescues hope they never have to enforce. Basically, if you turn out to be a rotten dog owner and someone tells rescue about it or if this is discovered by rescue in a follow-up visit, your dog can be taken away, permanently.

Now that all the paperwork is out of the way and you've signed on the dotted line, you'll be able to take your dog home. Make sure you have the essential equipment ready and waiting for your new dog: collar, leash, bed, crate, dog food (whatever the rescue is feeding), and food and water bowls. If you are uncertain as to what sizes or types of equipment to purchase, ask the breed rescue for advice in advance.

Follow-up Visits

If you think you've seen and heard the last of breed rescue on the day you get your dog, you're sorely mistaken! These people want to make sure that you and your dog are very happy together.

Most rescues will call within a few days to make sure things are going O.K. If things aren't, this is the perfect time to discuss with the rescue worker the problems you are having. Remember, there isn't a question that's too stupid to ask! These rescue people have seen it all and are more than happy to help you through any problems you might be having. In fact, it's a good idea to keep the rescue's phone number, along with the phone numbers of any other helpful dog people you've met along the way, in an easily accessible place.

Usually about a month after you've had the rescued dog, a rescue worker will schedule a home visit. During this visit, he or she will assess how well everyone is getting along, if the dog has adapted to its new home, if the dog is being properly taken care of, or if the initial situation has made a shift for the worse. The rescue worker may make some suggestions on how to solve some problem areas or, most likely, you'll get a big thumbs up for a job well done. Congratulations!

You now have a canine life partner. See, that wasn't so bad now, was it?

Tips on transitioning your new Greyhound to home life

1. Use a wire crate to help with housebreaking. (They're used to open crates and may feel confined by a closed-in travel crate.)
2. Carefully introduce your new dog to screens, windows and sliding glass doors.
3. Avoid any yummy treats for awhile. The adjustment from ground beef to dry food is always a shock to the dog's system and often results in diarrhea for several days.
4. Teach your dog how to go up steps by showing it how to go up some shallow, long steps (like at the library) first.
5. Never ever walk your dog off leash.
6. Allow your dog frequent high-paced run in a well-mowed, fenced field. As your new dog "becomes one" with the couch, you have to do this less and less.
7. Have patience! This is an intelligent dog, but there a lot of things it's never experienced before.
8. Your dog is used to being an early riser. Expect to rise early, too, for the initial few weeks.
9. Also expect to have a 60 - 80 lb shadow following you around the house continually for at least several weeks.
10. Make a nice soft bed indoors for your boney buddy.
11. Provide your new Greyhound with a quiet "escape," such as its crate. Home life can temporarily be overwhelming and the dog may want to stay by itself occasionally until it realizes it can be part of the family.

Williamson Kennels

There are 60 dogs at the Williamson Kennels at Tri-State Greyhound Park in Cross Lanes, W.V. and you can bet that every one of them adores Niva Williamson.

More than a decade ago, Ronnie Williamson, a retired police officer, cajoled his wife, Niva, into visiting the brand new Greyhound park across town. Reluctant at first, Niva eventually succombed to gentle prodding and went with her husband to watch the races. "I fell in love with the dogs," she says simply.

When an opportunity came available to purchase a kennel at the track, the Williamsons pooled their money and made the purchase. Today, they own a successful kennel at the track. "It's a lot of hard work," confesses Niva, a slender, blue-eyed, sharp-witted, 50-something woman who frequently puts in 14 -16 hour days with her husband. "And you've really got to love the dogs. You couldn't be in this business if you didn't."

A tour at the Williamson Kennels is enlightening: Every dog has a registered name, a "pet" name, and a particularly warm greeting for Niva. As I am introduced to each one, I feel as though I am meeting Niva's family. "She's a real sweetheart," Niva tells me as she gently rubs the ears of an elegant fawn brindle. "When she retires, I want to make sure she gets a really special home." She turns to a parti-colored male who won't quit barking. "Now, Luther, you'll get your turn," she laughs gently as she releases him from his crate. The young male is all wiggles and licks. "He just came to the track a few days ago. He's a really young dog."

Of course, there's one thing you can't help noticing at the Williamson Kennels. On the wall is a long row of little pieces of tape extending from the ceiling to the floor. On each piece of tape is a dog's name - the names of retired racers. In more than ten years of racing, Niva and Ronnie have never (that's right, never) euthanized a placeable dog. If a dog needed to have a bone set or required a special home and it took a month or two to find that home, the Williamsons paid the vet bills, fed and cared for that dog (often times not theirs but another owner's) until an appropriate home was located.

The Williamsons take great pride in their placement record, but Niva waves off the notion that they are doing anything special. "I don't think we're unusual," she says quietly. "We're just really fortunate to be able to work with some great placement organizations. We're just like any other kennel owners - we love our dogs. And we want them to all go to good homes."

CHAPTER 6

Dog Tracks and the Retired Greyhound - A Special Case

One of the largest Greyhound adoption studies was recently completed in which 880 Greyhound owners were surveyed on their experiences. The result? "Either the owners tolerated a lot - or this is one great dog," says Alan M. Beck, Sc.D., director of the Center for Applied Ethology and Human-Animal Interaction, Purdue University's School of Veterinary Medicine. "We found that there were less problems [with Greyhound adoptions] than one would normally expect. Of the 587 respondents, only 13 people reported having returned their dogs. That's an amazingly low number. It's something to say in itself for the dog coming off the track."

Bob Jahn, director of REGAP (Retired Greyhounds As Pets) of Indianapolis, Indiana, says these numbers sound about right. Placing Greyhounds since 1987, Jahn says that few dogs ever are returned. "If a dog is returned, it's usually not the dog's fault. Divorce, a lost job, failed health, a move to a smaller place that doesn't allow large dogs--these are the reasons we see most often."

Loving, gentle and calm, Greyhounds make wonderful family dogs. They are quiet, well-mannered and require little training to adjust to a life of luxury as a pet. They are tall but after a while, you don't even notice this. Greyhounds are not high-strung nor do they have a high activity level. They are primarily couch potatoes except for a five to ten minute burst of high-speed frolicking that is best done a couple days a week in a large, fenced field. Greyhounds have an affinity for soft, cushy places (couches and beds) and the ability to forever hold a place in your heart.

Transitioning from track to home is not particularly difficult for the dogs either, but the experience is a little unique for the adoptive owner. "It's like having an innocent puppy that's never experienced anything except that puppy is in a big dog's body," laughs Denise Davis, founder of Greyhound Rescue, Inc. in Elkridge, Maryland, who has placed well over 1,000 Greyhounds in the last seven years. "They've never had to go up and down stairs before, so you have to teach them. They've never seen a screen, large windows or sliding glass doors and will try to run right through them unless you show them what they are. They don't know they're not supposed to jump up on the dining room table and grab the dinner roast," explains Davis. "But they're very intelligent and eager to please. It doesn't take long to teach them the rules. At most, maybe two months. The more you're willing to put in, the more you'll get out."

In order to more fully understand the retired Greyhound and be able to decide if this is the dog you'd really like to adopt, most placement organizations stress that it is particularly important to understand the history of the breed and receive an honest view of life on the track.

A Little Breed History

Greyhounds are an ancient breed. Dating back to the times of the Egyptians, the noble Greyhound has been a loyal sporting companion to its master for thousands of years. Ownership of the Greyhound has historically been a treasured one, a right reserved for royalty.

In England, the sport of hare coursing (chasing and catching a live hare in an open field) was popular even as early as Saxon times. A keen-sighted, agile and fast runner with early speed was naturally a prized possession and a carefully guarded commodity. Laws were actually enacted to punish commoners who had the temerity to have a Greyhound in their possession. In 1776, Great Britain's first coursing club was formed along with a set of rules to determine the winners of this increasingly popular sport. During the latter 1700s and 1800s, Greyhound coursing events were known as the "sport of queens."

In the United States, the sport of coursing and racing grew from "necessity." Overrun with vermin, farmers in the Midwest turned to the Greyhound to get the problem under control. It wasn't long before farmers were trying to answer the question as to whose dog could hunt the best and which one was fastest. Two racing societies grew from these grass-roots beginnings.

Hare coursing, a close cousin to the coursing events of old, was an obvious branch into competitive sports for Greyhounds in the United States. Still popular today in such states as California, open field coursing involves the pursuit (and early demise) of a live jack rabbit.

However, the sport has its pitfalls. Not all terrain in all areas of the country is suited to this sport.

Additionally, over the years, many states have outlawed the use of live animals (rabbits) in this manner. So, avid coursers began looking for another way to race their dogs that would have national appeal.

Lure coursing, which involves the chasing of an artificial lure strung on a complex pulley system, made its entrance in the late 1960s and continues to be popular today. The many twists and turns of the course closely imitate the unpredictable and erratic running style of the hare. The course can generally be easily set up in a large field or even a recreational park (polo fields, soccer fields, etc.). Greyhounds, along with other members of the sighthound group (Afghan Hounds, Borzois, Salukis, Whippets, etc.), are the only breeds eligible to compete in this sport. It is an amateur sport designed for the enjoyment of both owner and dog. No parimutuel betting is allowed; the rewards for a course well run are trophies and potentially points toward a lure coursing championship. Both the American Sighthound Field Association and the American Kennel Club sanction lure coursing events across the country. If you adopt a retired racer, be sure to give this fun sport a whirl. Your dog will absolutely love it!

Meanwhile, another faction of Greyhound owners was developing a slightly different sport--track racing. As with lure coursing, the dogs are trained to chase an artificial lure; however, the course is neither erratic nor in an open field. Instead, the Greyhounds are provided with a deep, soft dirt track much like a horse track, oval in shape, and 1/4 mile long. The first parimutuel dog track was opened in the 1920s, but it wasn't until the 1970s and 1980s that Greyhound racing really took off in a very big way. Today, Greyhound racing faces stiff competition for gambling dollars and is not nearly as profitable a business as it once was. There are currently 50 tracks operating in 15 states.

The Down Side of Track Life

Few people haven't been exposed to the "plight of the Greyhound." In the mid-1980s, there were several atrocities within the dog racing industry that received national attention. The world was shocked and the industry was shaken.

However, it is important to remember that incidents such as these are not unique nor are they limited to the Greyhound industry. Mistreatment of animals is not limited to working dogs, but extends deep into our society and covers all strata of social levels and all sorts of animal-human relationships. Simply said, there are bad apples in every crop of humans. There are men who batter their wives, mothers who shake their babies, farmers who neglect their livestock, and pet owners who are cruel to their dogs. How someone could ever cause injury to an animal or person that is so loving and virtually defenseless, is a question that no one has been able to answer yet.

However, as far as the Greyhound industry is concerned, Beck makes an important observation:

"There are abuses in everything but a willingness to minimize them and respond and repair is all we can ask any endeavor." And respond and repair is exactly what the Greyhound industry did.

The National Greyhound Association (NGA) and Track Operators Association immediately took serious measures and clamped down to minimize any further mistreatment or neglect of these graceful, elegant animals. The American Greyhound Council was formed in 1987 with the explicit purpose of dealing with animal welfare issues and the general care of the track Greyhound, both while at puppy farms and when racing at the tracks.

Today, every large puppy farm (20 puppies or more) is inspected at least once a year. Small farms (one or two litters a year) can count on an inspection within a two year period. "If anything is found to be inadequate, and that doesn't mean life threatening, the farm owner is given 30 days to rectify the situation," says Gary Guccione, secretary and treasurer of the NGA and executive editor of The Greyhound Review. "If, when the inspectors return, the farm is not up to standards a hearing is held and they could be barred." To be barred from the Greyhound industry is no light slap on the wrist; it is a lifetime penalty that prevent the barred person from having anything to do with Greyhounds for the rest of their lives.

Restrictions are equally as tight at the tracks. Simply stated, mistreatment, neglect or abuse of dogs is plainly not tolerated at the tracks and those who do break the rules are barred from the sport for life. Not only are these people forbidden to have anything to do with Greyhounds, but other Greyhound people are likewise forbidden to have anything to do with the barred members, otherwise, they risk being barred themselves.

What is considered mistreatment? According to Guccione, it could be something such as physical abuse (don't you wish you had that kind of control over pet owners?), feeding the dogs inadequately, or not maintaining sanitary kennels (which could include missing a turn-out one morning).

Kennel owners are subject to scheduled inspections as well as "spot" inspections. Track officials and state officials routinely make scheduled and unscheduled inspections of the kennels at the track. Added to these inspections are occasional visits from the American Greyhound Council inspectors. In addition, dogs are regularly examined by the track veterinarian (who is not a track employee but is an employee of the state) every time the dogs "cross the scales" or "weigh in" before a race. The track vet looks for tell-tale signs of neglect or abuse and can file a report, launch an investigation, or make a spot kennel inspection.

In addition, the kennel owners keep an eye out for the dogs themselves. "When you sometimes run into trouble is when there is an absentee kennel owner who isn't around to check up on his employees," says one respected kennel owner who preferred to remain unnamed. "If we see someone's missed cleaning their kennels one morning or if we hear a tone of voice that isn't appropriate, you can bet someone reports it."

Today, mistreatment of the dogs is really not that common. Davis, who makes frequent trips to tracks through her placement program, says, "You hear these rumors about things going on at the track, and they're usually from someone who's never been there. I go to the track all the time and I've just not seen it. I'm sure there are some bad kennel owners, just like there are some bad pet owners, but I've never seen any mistreatment at the track."

Guccione points out that it just wouldn't make sense for a kennel owner to mistreat a dog that is the source of his or her livelihood. "A racing Greyhound is a substantial investment. On average, it takes $2,500 to get a dog to the point where it is ready to run its first race." Guccione adds that there's no room for mistreatment in this business, "You can't take shortcuts and expect the dogs to run well. Everyone knows that."

Of course, there are always those individuals who defy any common sense. As Beck points out that, "Productivity, whether it be in meat or egg production, or racing speed for horses or dogs, is not necessarily an indicator of good husbandry anymore than child labor is an indication that the children are happy and healthy."

But to credit the NGA for the great strides that have been made, there are statistics that indicate things are really looking up for the Greyhound. In the last ten years (which includes the mid-80s with their well-publicized "atrocities"), there have been less than three incidents a year that have required the NGA to barr a member. When you consider that in a given year there are 50,000 adult dogs on the track and another 30,000 puppies in various stages of playing or training, 2.7incidents of neglect or abuse is actually a pretty minimal figure.

Despite all of the NGA's efforts and the good, honest hard work that is being done everyday by the majority of kennel owners, the Greyhound industry is still an easy target. Wild, unfounded rumors still run rampant and really need to be put to rest. The following are ten of the misconceptions most frequently heard by placement organizations.

Top 10 List of Fiction, False Rumors and Hogwash
Fable #1. Greyhound racing is a cruel sport.

Truly bogus. The dogs absolutely live for running. If you decide to adopt a retired racer, you will quickly find this out! Greyhounds are true canine athletes and have been bred to want to run and chase for literally thousands of years! In fact, if a person were to adopt a retired Greyhound with the notion that they were going to save the dog from a life of running, they would be in for a big surprise. If a retired Greyhound is not allowed a high-speed romp once or twice a week in an enclosed field, you'll have a very sad Greyhound indeed.

Fable #2. Greyhounds are isolated and poorly socialized.

There's no possible way a dog could come off the track and have such a good attitude toward other dogs and people if it had been deprived of regular, healthy human and canine contact.

"Their whole life is a continual puppy party," says Beck. "It's safe to say that these Greyhounds get much more attention than we give most our pets. The dog that is left alone all day while we're at work is not going to have the amount of attention a track dog gets. A Greyhound's life is highly social."

If you ever spend a day at the track, you would appreciate just how much loving attention these dogs get. Things are very busy around the racing kennels from early in the morning (first turnout is at 6 a.m.) until the final turnout at 10 p.m. The dogs are all handled, petted, played with, and praised profusely for performing their morning training workouts on a daily basis. They are bathed, groomed, get their ears cleaned and toenails clipped on a regular basis. In other words, except for perhaps one or two hours in the day, the dogs are constantly interacting with humans.

Additionally, dog-aggression is rarely a problem with Greyhounds. As a rule, the dogs are generally very sociable with their running mates.

Fable #3. Greyhounds are fed poor quality, inferior food at the track:

These dogs are like finely-tuned racing cars: they just don't run on cheap fuel. They are high- octane models! The meals I have seen prepared for Greyhounds rival the most gourmet, home-cooked dog meal you could imagine! Some kennels use very high-grade name brand dog food (the same as I use!), while others mix their own special ingredients, consisting of fresh ground beef, garlic, cabbage (or other steamed vegetables), applesauce, and a healthy serving of high-grade dry dog food.

And, no, the dogs are not starved. For a dog to be in peak running shape, the last three ribs will show when the dog is breathing hard. Much like a human runner, there is a tremendous amount of muscle (which would not be there if the dog were underfed) and not much fat.

Fable #4. Track dogs don't receive proper veterinary care.

All dogs at the track are required to be current on their vaccinations. In addition, kennel owners keep a keen eye on the dogs' general health. These animals are performance athletes and, just like their human counterparts, require a lot of special attention to keep healthy, injury-free and in peak condition.

Fable #5. Greyhounds are brutally killed.

The NGA requires that any Greyhound that is euthanized must be put to sleep in a manner approved by the American Veterinary Medical Association. "In fact." Guccione points out, "we don't even accept all the methods approved by the American Veterinary Medical Association. [The NGA] requires that all Greyhounds are euthanized by a veterinarian with a painless, lethal injection." No gun shots, no clubbings, or anything else horrible that you've probably heard is allowed. Anyone who uses an unacceptable alternative method of euthanasia will be barred for life from track racing.

Fable #6. Greyhounds don't bark because they're muzzled at the track.

This is absurd. If anyone tells you this, it is obvious that they know very little about the breed.

The fact that Greyhounds don't bark much has nothing to do with muzzling. Greyhounds are sighthounds, a group of dogs which by nature doesn't bark a whole heck of a lot. "If a Greyhound barks, it's usually because it's excited or it wants to play," says Davis. "They make lousy guard dogs . . ."

Additionally, the muzzles used at the track are very open, allowing the dogs to drink with their (turn out) muzzles on, or take in all the air they want (with their racing muzzles on). The dogs wear their muzzles when they are racing to identify whose nose crossed the finish line first. They wear their muzzles in the turn-out pens just in case a new dog wants to start a little squabble.

Both styles of muzzles allow the dogs to bark up a storm if they want to.

Fable #7. Track dogs are cruelly confined.

This rumor probably originated from someone who had never visited a racing kennels or was an anti-crating activitist. There are approximately 70 dogs in a kennel each with its own crate. No crates are shared. The crates that are built by the track for the dogs are downright spacious. They are open-mesh, allowing the dogs to see everything that is going on. The bedding, which is changed daily, usually is a thick layer of shredded newspaper, allowing the dogs to build a fluffy nest. Often the dogs will have a favorite toy, one of those plush animals, in their crate to snuggle with, too.

Additionally, the dogs are let out to romp and relieve themselves at least four or five times during the course of the day. Several times a week, the dogs get a chance to cut loose and run. A real treat for these guys. If you ever get an opportunity to see a dog that has just come off the track, you'll very quickly realize that the dogs are receiving adequate exercise!

Fable #8. Track dogs are poorly-bred and have a lot of genetic problems.

Track Greyhounds are probably one of the healthiest, longest-lived large breed of dog in existence. Whereas a dog of similar stature may only live to be 8-years-old, the Greyhound can be expected to live up to 12 years or longer with few problems. "There are exceptions," says Jahn, "But I would say the norm is 12, 13, 14 years or more."

In addition, Greyhounds have few congenital problems. Jahn relates that he had a well- known Greyhound trainer of 30 years turn to him one day and ask, "So what is this hip dysplasia thing I hear that other dogs get? I've never seen it." Other problems such as blindness, deafness, epilepsy, allergies, skin disorders, congenital heart problems, ear infections and other common maladies are virtually unheard of in Greyhounds. "The only problems you might see are thyroid disorders and the fact that the dog's got thin skin which tears very easily." Jahn adds that the thyroid disorder is generally not life-threatening and often costs as little as 10 cents a day to treat.

Fable #9. When a track closes, eight hundred dogs are killed.

If a horse track were closed, do you think every horse in the stables would be shot? Not hardly. Greyhounds move from track to track just as Thoroughbreds do. Some dog tracks run higher graded races than others, so the faster dogs work their way up to those tracks. Similarly, a slower dog may have many chances at several tracks to do well before it gets moved to the lowest graded track. The number of dogs that need homes when a track closes depends largely on the quality of the track. For example, when the track in Bridgeport, Connecticut closed recently, of the 800 or so dogs at the track, nearly all of them moved to other tracks. Only 40 Greyhounds needed to be placed.

Davis adds that when a "bottom rung" track recently closed, the NGA stepped in and made sure that every placeable dog (roughly 200 or so) found a good home. "They even made arrangements to ship some dogs to the East Coast to several placement agencies here. That's impressive."

Fable #10. Track dogs are given dangerous levels of performance enhancement drugs.

Steroids are given to female dogs but not in quantities meant to enhance muscle bulk. Rather, the steroids' purpose is to prevent the lovely ladies from coming into season. Imagine the turmoil of a 60-dog kennel if 15 females were in season at once! In addition, winning track Greyhounds are routinely screened with a urinalysis for the presence of any forms of illegal substances.

The Real Problem with Dog Tracks

While the dogs are being reared or running on the track, life is good. However, even the fastest dog begins to loose its speed by the age of five. That's less than half a lifetime. Others wash out as young as two years old. Unfortunately for these gentle athletes, there are no "retirement" farms. If a home cannot be found for the ex-racer, it is euthanized.

Approximately 28,000 dogs came off the track in 1995. Of those dogs, 16,000 were placed in homes. The remaining 12,000 dogs were euthanized. This is a number of which the racing industry is fervently trying to reduce. "Since 1992, we've been able to reduce the number of dogs coming onto the tracks by one third," says Guccione. "In 1992, more than 50,000 puppies registered. This year [1996], our numbers are closer to 34,000. The NGA has been putting a lot of pressure on the breeders. We want puppy farms to concentrate on quality not quantity." In addition to continuing to bring the breeding numbers down, the NGA has also worked hard to encourage dog owners, kennel owners and the tracks themselves to accept personal responsibility to find homes for the retired Greyhounds. "Every track in the United States now either has its own, on-site placement kennels which is funded by dog owners, kennel owners and the track or the track has several rescue organizations with which it works closely. Our ultimate goal is to place all adoptable Greyhounds into a pet program. It's a doable thing."

An interesting point to note: The tracks work with a wide range of rescue groups, including those that are fighting to have the entire industry abolished. "That just goes to show you how much we care about the dogs," says Guccione. "It's more important for us to find homes for these wonderful dogs than it is for us to agree."

Life as a track dog

Greyhound puppies may be whelped by breeders, dog owners, kennel owners or those who operate puppy farms (not to be confused with puppy mills!) in what is commonly referred to as a nursery. About a month after the pups are weaned from their mother, they are tattooed. The right ear's sequence of numbers indicates the month and year the pup was born. The letter at the end represents the birth order (i.e., "B" is 2nd). The left ear is the pup's NGA registration number.

At four months of age, the gangly Greyhound puppies generally move to a "rearing facility" more commonly called a puppy farm. Mostly a place for play and lots of running, puppy farms provide young pups with socialization and some preliminary training. The young puppies are encouraged to chase and "kill" stuffed animals and other fluffy toys. In addition, they receive lots of gentle handling and are trained to walk on a leash.

When the pup is about a year old, it is sent to a training center where it will spend four to six months learning the ropes of racing, including how to break out of a starting box, get used to wearing a muzzle, and run with other dogs. All young racers are trained on artificial lures. Some may also be trained on live hares; however, this practice is illegal in most states and not condoned by the NGA. Regardless of how it is trained, a track dog will nearly always chase a small, moving furry object. ("In an open field, dogs chase cats . . . Greyhounds catch them," comments Jahn. "Indoors, with proper training and introduction, there's usually not a problem.")

Once the dog has successfully completed its training, it is sent to a Greyhound track. The dog is usually around 16- to 18-months-old when it gets to run its first race. Interestingly, an owner cannot simply drive up to the track, run his dog and then go home. In order for the dog to run at a track, the owner must find an opening at one of the many track kennels on the premises. Tracks generally have ten kennels that are owned and run by independent kennel owners. Each kennel has its own trainer(s) and employees. Many kennel owners board and train their own dogs, but the majority of the Greyhounds in the kennel (up to 70% or more) are "leased" dogs. The kennel owner is responsible for the care and training of the leased dogs as well as their own crew.

Track kennels have 24-hour security to prevent anyone from intentionally (or unintentionally) trying to harm, tamper with or steal the dogs. The kennels are not open to the general public but are, as noted earlier, frequently inspected by a host of officials. Before a person can work for one of the track kennels, he or she must undergo a background check which includes a search for violations of the NGA's regulations.

Mornings are early at the track, with the first turn-out coming at 6 a.m. The Greyhounds are housed in large, sturdy crates which line the walls of the kennel and form a single crate aisle down the middle. The kennels are air conditioned and heated, keeping a comfortable temperate climate for the dogs. Outside, the turn-out pens are large and filled with thick sand. In each pen, fresh buckets are put out for the dogs to drink from before and after they relieve themselves.

Females go in one pen and males go in another. The dogs are turned out ten or so at a time with an attentive employee cleaning up after each batch of dogs. While the dogs are out of their crates, another employee is busy changing bedding and scrubbing down the floors. This entire process can take up to two hours.

Once all the dogs have been turned out, it's time for morning sprints. The dogs know this and often begin barking and singing (Yes, it's quite a chorus!) in excitement. Not every dog gets to run every day, so it's a real treat to be chosen. The trainer takes a few dogs at a time to a long, enclosed straight sprint track. Basically, the dogs run back and forth between the trainer and whomever is helping him, many times the kennel owner. On other days, the kennel may have track time reserved and are able to work with their dogs on the oval track itself. Owners are regularly kept advised of their dogs' progress and of the dogs' race entries.

On race day, the dog is given a good rubdown so that its coat is clean and glossy. (Gotta look good for the winner's circle photo, right?) The dog is weighed and the weight is provided by the trainer in the dog's race entry. The dog's weight must not vary by more than 1 1/2 pounds at race time, or it will be scratched. The dogs that will be in the evening's racing program are driven over and dropped off at the track's holding kennel two hours before the racing program begins. There, they must wait until post time.

The second turnout of the day is at 10 a.m. The same process is followed as in the 6 a.m. turnout except instead of changing the bedding, the employees (or kennel owner or trainer) are busily mixing up a winning concoction of food. The actual feeding of the dogs is a science in itself and generally takes place after all the dogs have finished with their turnouts. Each dog's serving is carefully weighed to keep the dog in peak condition and at its optimum running weight. Then, the dog's own particular mixture of supplements is added to the meal. Feeding 70 dogs with this kind of specificity takes time and the din that comes from this many hungry dogs is, well, loud.

Once the dogs have finished eating and all the bowls are picked up, it's rest time. The lights are turned out, the music is turned up a little bit, and everyone takes a little break from the dogs. Not a long break, however, because the next turnout is scheduled to begin in the early afternoon and again at 8 p.m.

On race days, which are usually six out of seven days, the kennel owners and trainers watch each of their dogs' races, carefully noting how the dog broke from the starting box, how it ran its race, and how it finished. Kennel owners are paid by a point system; the higher the dog's placing in the race, the more points it wins. Also, the higher grade race it is in, the more points each place is worth. In other words, a dog winning an "A" race will receive more points than a dog that wins a "D" race. The kennel owner's total points for the week are calculated along with the total amount of revenues brought in by the track. One week, a point may be worth $40. Another week, that same point may be worth $60.

After the conclusion of the evening's last race, the kennel owners and trainers make sure the dogs are all safely returned to their kennels and that all other chores have been completed. By 10 or 11 o'clock, the kennel owner's long day usually comes to an end.

Adopting a retired racer from the track

One of the ways you can adopt a retired Greyhound is often the most overlooked method:

Directly from the Greyhound race track. More and more tracks are organizing "on-site" adoption kennels. (See Appendix B: Sources for Adult Greyhounds - Tracks and Rescue Organizations for race tracks that currently offer this option.) Adopting a dog directly from the track is a great way not only to see the dogs run (you should catch a race or two) but also a way in which you can more thoroughly understand the track lifestyle. For example, when you see the openness of the crates, you'll understand why most placement people encourage you to use open mesh crates at home instead of the closed-in travel crates. You'll also notice that music plays all the time in the kennels, something which you can use at home to help your canine Thoroughbred make a smooth transition. And you'll also be able to meet some of the track folks.

One of the greatest advantages of going directly to the track to select your Greyhound is that you have so many dogs to choose from - probably 50 - 90 at one time. (Of course, this can have its disadvantages, too. Which one to pick?) Another advantage is that the people who run the track placement programs are Greyhound people. They eat, sleep and breathe Greyhounds. There isn't a question in this world you could ask that they wouldn't know or wouldn't be able to get the answer for you.

A word of warning, however. Don't go to the track thinking you can walk in, get a dog and walk out. You will be screened and you will be required to wait at least a week to ten days before you can pick up your dog.

Also, it's not a good idea to adopt a dog from a track if the track is not close to where you live unless, of course, you're an experienced Greyhound owner. "You'd be surprised how many people go down to Florida on vacation, apply for a dog the day they get there and bring it back with them when they return home," says Davis. "Now they've got this dog home and they don't have a local support network to help them through the adjustment period."

"I've had Florida tracks call me before to ask me to help them," relates Jahn. "They'll call and say that the dog is in Indiana and the owners need help. I've had dogs returned to me that orignated from another state."

So, be careful. If you do adopt from out-of-state, Davis recommends immediately hooking up with a local rescue for advice and information.

Working with a Greyhound Track

If you are nearby a dog track and want to go through the track's adoption program, the first step is to call the program director and discuss their adoption process. Most programs are run similarly to a breed rescue organization and will begin by interviewing you over the telephone.

Placement director Sonya Lambert at Tri-State Race Track in Cross Lanes, W.V., explains that the interview is an initial screening of the applicant. "We want to know why you are interested in adopting an adult dog and we are very concerned that the dog goes to a good home. We don't allow dogs to be given as gifts."

If you pass initial muster, you will be required to fill out an adoption application. You will be asked questions about your dog experience, your lifestyle, why you want a Greyhound , if you have any other pets (be sure to note on the app if you have a cat.), etc. In the second half of the application, you will be asked what you are looking for in a Greyhound, what color, what sex, preferred age, and so on. Warning! Don't get your heart set on a particular color, unless it's black, fawn or brindle which are the most common. If you prefer a more unusual color, such as blue or a white parti-color, you may have to wait a little while. It's O.K. to note what you prefer, but keep your mind and heart open to the best dog for your situation. Also, it is very important that you fill out this application honestly so that the placement director can make the best match possible.

After you've mailed in the application, the rescue coordinator will most likely call you and go over your answers. If there are any problems (i.e., no fenced yard), the program director may discuss what you are willing to do to rectify the situation. Once your application has been approved, you will be able to schedule a visit to meet the dogs. If you have children, bring 'em along. Make sure you let the kids know you are just looking.

When you arrive at the track, the placement director will have to clear you through security before you can go back to the kennels, so you'll need to check in at the guard gate. At this time, you will most likely be greeted by the director and escorted back to the placement kennels.

When the kennel door is finally opened and the lights turned on, expect to be greeted by a din of jubilant barking.

Usually, the placement director will have five or six males and the same number of females for you to take a look at. Even though there may be 60 dogs in the kennels, the hand-picked ones are the dogs that the placement director feels will best fit your lifestyle. You will be able to play with the dogs one-on-one in the kennels and in the turn-out pen.

Once you've made a decision as to which dog you'd like (or when a dog has picked you out - which is much more often the case), you will need to pay the adoption fee (which covers the spay/neuter) and sign a simple adoption contract. You do not get to pick up your dog at this visit!

The selected dog will be taken to the vet to have its spay/neuter performed and then allowed to heal in the kennels.

About a week after your initial visit, you will be allowed to pick up your retired racer and take it home. Be sure to have all the basic "dog" necessities ready before your Greyhound comes home: Dog food, bowls, a comfy bed, leash, and a hound collar. A Greyhound's head is smaller than its neck and, therefore, they are quite adept at giving their heads a little toss and pulling backwards to get out of their collars. Hound collars are available in most stores and are well worth the investment.

Once you've brought your Greyhound home, be sure to keep in contact with the placement kennels. They've heard and seen it all. So, no question is too frivolous or should ever be considered "stupid." Just ask. You'll be glad you did.

Adoptions through Greyhound Rescue Organizations

An anomaly just a decade ago, there are now literally scores of Greyhound rescues across the country. Greyhound rescuers come in all shapes and sizes and everyone has their own methods of screening and placing dogs. Some groups are very stringent and unyielding; others are more interested in finding good homes for these great dogs and will work with you to make your situation perfect. The rescue should always be willing to take back the dog if things don't work out for any reason.

A good rescuer is pleasant, upbeat and will ask a lot of questions of you. Please don't be intimidated or insulted by all these questions - they are asked for the good of the dog. "You just can't be too careful," says Jahn. "I can remember placing a dog with a Cambodian family. I think it was only the second batch of dogs that I had placed." Jahn pauses, poignantly. "We're pretty sure they ate the dog. So, you can sort of understand why we're cautious."

If you don't feel comfortable with the group you are working with or if you feel awkward asking for help or advice, try another rescue group. Depending on where you live, however, you may not have much choice.

Once you've found a rescue group that you are comfortable with, you can expect to go through the same process of adoption as described in Chapter 3: Purebred Rescue. You'll be expected to fill out an adoption questionnaire, endure a phone interview, and make a visit to the placement director's home (or a Greyhound Fair) to meet and play with the dogs. When your app is approved, you may be put on a waiting list. Many rescue groups wait until they have several applications and then make a trip to pick up dogs from the track. Other groups may regularly pick up dogs and, in this instance, may have one perfectly suited for you that is available immediately.

Once your dog match is made, you will get the opportunity to meet it before taking it home.

Many times, the dogs will come off the track unsprayed or not neutered, so you may have to wait again as your dog has this surgery performed. When you and your dog have gotten through all of this, it is finally time to bring the lucky dog home. But don't expect the process to be quite over yet. You will receive follow-up calls from the rescue group. Be sure to ask any questions that you have or discuss any problems you are having with the rescue group at this time. They should be a great source of help to you. You may also receive a follow-up visit or a "spot check," as well.

But wait! You're not still not through. Greyhound owners are usually congenial sorts (much like the dogs they own) and are big on holding annual picnics, monthly fun runs and play groups. Don't hesitate to get active! It's a lot of fun to meet other owners and it's very rewarding to see so many happy, rescued dogs living in the lap of luxury as a house dog.

And, after you've had your hound for awhile, why not consider adding a second one? If you don't mind the two making a mini-racetrack in your living room or backyard, having two truly is double the fun!

CHAPTER 7
Pounds, Shelters and Other Sources

The most common way to adopt an adult dog is to walk down to the local shelter or pound on a Saturday morning, take a look at the dogs, pay the director $25 and go home with a new dog. No fuss, no muss. Really easy, right? Wrong. Picking out the perfect preowned pet from a shelter can be one of the most difficult ways to select a dog. Your level of success often depends on the quality of the shelter and the dedication of the staff. However, if you understand how pounds, shelters and other agencies operate and come prepared and educated as to how to select a dog in this type of situation, you will greatly increase your odds of making a wonderful selection.

The Worst Case Scenario

The noise, confusion and sheer number of animals housed side by side (or together, in some instances) can create an almost overwhelming situation for some dogs. The big dogs intimidate the little dogs. There are fights and frights. Some shelters are very small and pack multiple dogs to a run. When a dog is overwhelmed, frightened or sick, it is extremely difficult to determine the canine's true temperament. The pound or shelter experience can be quite traumatic to even the most congenial dog. A dog that would generally be plucky and bouncy in a home situation might respond to being kenneled alongside or with strangers in a very negative way, cowering in the back of the crate or even acting aggressively. Potential adopters generally try to avoid dogs displaying these types of behavior. And for good reason! However, many times an adoptable dog is overlooked because it is displaying the wrong behaviors at the wrong time.

If the confusion of a shelter isn't enough to discourage an adoption, sometimes the lack of assistance can be. If a shelter is underfinanced, the facility isn't going to offer all the luxuries of a well-funded, richly supported shelter. Translated, that means you won't be screened, you won't be assisted in your selection, and the dogs will not be vet checked, evaluated for temperament, or spayed or neutered. In this type of scenario, it is extremely difficult to determine much of anything about a dog's temperament or even its general health.

Often running hand in hand with a lack of funds is a lack of shelter workers and/or volunteers. If a shelter is short on staff, the staff is likely to be "short." Being overworked and underpaid doesn't help to make the situation any better. Nor does the job itself. In fact, working at a shelter can be one of the hardest jobs around emotionally. Think about it. Can you even imagine having to go to work every day knowing that you'll have to euthanize most of the dogs that you've worked so hard to rescue, nurture and befriend?

And finally, regardless of the quality of the shelter, where there are dogs, there is noise. Lots of noise. Imagine walking into a room filled with 1,000 dogs--all barking. Some of the larger cities have shelters that truly are this large. But even if the shelter houses 60 or 70 dogs, it's still noisy.

In the din, it's hard to hear what shelter workers are telling you about the dogs. In fact, it may be hard to even get a worker's attention.

A Better Picture

So what's a person to do? First of all, there is good news. According to Lynn Stulberg, D.V.M., director of PETsMART's Luv-a-Pet Program and PETsMART Charities, the good adoption agencies outnumber the bad. Stulberg, who is in part responsible for the screening of all adoption agencies that want to participate in the pet fairs held at PETsMART's 300+ locations, is very familiar with the quality of adoption agencies nationwide. "We work with nearly a thousand adoption organizations across the country, both government-run and nonprofit, through our Luv-a-Pet program. In the many years that we have been offering this adoption program, most organizations meet our screening standards," testifies Stulberg. "Overall, there are a lot of really good people doing tremendous work in the animal adoption field."

Nationally, the shelter scene can run the range of limits from ultra-modern facilities with a seemingly never ending supply of funds, to buildings that are barely standing and an annual report that always runs in the red. You'll find shelters in which the dogs receive home cooked meals, listen to tranquil music, receive massages and perhaps are even indulged with Bach Flower remedies to calm their nerves, while elsewhere there are dogs in other shelters that are lucky if their kennels are cleaned once a day. Some shelters carefully screen prospective owners.

Others are thankful just to place another dog. Regardless, there are two things all of these shelters have in common: adoptable dogs and the unified goal to find homes for these dogs. In your area, you may not have a big choice as to what kinds of shelters are available. But, if you'd like to adopt a dog through the shelter system, it's handy to know what kinds of shelters are out there and what their adoption policies are. In this way, you can be better equipped to know how to choose a dog.

Types of Facilities

Pounds

This is the municipally run animal control facility. At one time or another in our lives, we've probably all seen the dog catcher out trying to capture a stray dog. The "pound" is where these stray dogs often end up if they are caught. If the dog is wearing identification tags, the owner is called and given the opportunity to pick up the dog. If the dog does not have an identification tag, it is tagged (sometimes a very sticky numbered sticker on the hip) by the pound. The dog then goes to a holding area. If a dog is not claimed by its owner within a certain amount of time, usually two or three days, the dog is moved into the adoption pens. This stay is relatively short. If no one adopts the dog by the time it has moved to the "on deck" pen, the dog is euthanized. Dogs at the pound may be flea and tick dipped to prevent the spread of disease but, for obvious reasons, are not spayed or neutered nor are they vet checked or vaccinated.

Generally speaking, there are little or no adoption related services at the pound. In fact, depending on the community's anti-discrimination sensitivity, the pound employees may not be able to provide screening, counseling and/or placement services. The pound employee, in many instances, must release the dog to the "adopter," regardless of whether this person will provide a good home or not) or risk being sued for discrimination. (There are exceptions to every rule, however! See "Joint Efforts" below.)

Shelters

A shelter may be municipally run or it may be operated by a nonprofit organization. Nonprofit shelters may be government run, locally operated by a nonprofit agency, or they might be affiliated with a national effort, such as the Humane Society or Society for the Prevention of Cruelty to Animals. Shelter workers at government facilities are paid staff, whereas, employees at nonprofit facilities are usually a combination of paid staff and volunteers.

Some shelters actively pick up stray dogs and rescue abused canines. Other shelters limit their adoption services to owner surrendered pets and dogs that have been abandoned at veterinarian offices, dog groomers and boarding kennels. Yes, there are people who actually "leave" their dogs and never return. Or pay the bill. Conditions at shelters are usually a little better than at the pounds, with most facilities providing individual runs or crates to the rescued animals.

Some shelters call themselves "no-kill" shelters. The policy at these shelters is to place all adoptable dogs. When the runs are full, no more dogs are accepted. However, the term "no-kill" is somewhat of a misnomer. All shelters euthanize animals. What separates kill and no-kill shelters are the reasons why the dogs are euthanized. A "no-kill" shelter euthanizes only those dogs that are terminally ill or have poor temperaments. However, when the no-kill shelter is full (which is a common occurrence), animals have to be turned away to unknown but often predictable and painful - destinies. A "kill" shelter, on the other hand, will not only euthanize for health and temperament reasons, but will also euthanize dogs after a certain period of time if the dog has not been adopted out.

Regardless of whether the shelter is kill or no-kill, city run or private nonprofit, volunteer staffed or paid employees, all shelters are in the business of rescuing and finding homes for the animals in their care.

The Vanderburgh Humane Society (VHS) in Evansville, Indiana is a good example of how a well-run shelter operates. The 200-animal shelter is located in the heartland of America and is a pioneer in many aspects. "Dogs with special needs or those who just need a little TLC are placed in foster homes," explains Rachael Wilhite, public relations and humane education manager of VHS. One of the VHS' foster families recently cared for a litter of five puppies. "If the dog is sick, has little ones or is just overwhelmed, we try to find a foster home for them."

The VHS also offers a full range of adoption services. Owners surrendering their animals must fill out a "personality profile" on the dog and are required to pay at a minimum a $5 fee to help offset vaccination costs. Staff members frequently follow this up with their own temperament analysis. The surrendered dog then receives a complete check up from a veterinary technician along with blood and stool tests, worming where necessary, and a battery of shots and vaccinations. The dog is then "held" for a period of seven to ten days in which the dog is observed. If all has gone well, the dog is ready to be adopted. Interested adopters receive selection assistance from the staff members and are allowed to take the dog away from the facility on a walk. If the owner already has a dog at home, he or she is encouraged to bring the dog with them to see if the two dogs will get along.

Once a dog has been selected, the person is asked to fill out an application. "One of our staff members will go over the completed application with the applicant," says Wilhite. "Sometimes we will request a home visit, too. If the individual refuses the home visit, we won't adopt the dog out."

When an adopter is approved for a dog, he or she not only receives a great dog (usually an "American" dog, one with a melting pot lineage), but also such extras as a voucher for a spay/neuter (included in the $65 adoption fee) and a free initial veterinarian checkup. VHS, along with all rescue organizations, takes its spay/neuter contract very seriously: "If the new owner doesn't have their dog spayed or neutered within 30 days after adopting the pet, our field investigator calls them. If they haven't completed the spay/neuter after three follow-up calls or visits, we can legally seize the dog."

Of course, once the dog goes home with its new owner, VHS does not fade out of the picture.

"We are always available for follow-up advice and help," says Wilhite. "We encourage people to call anytime." The shelter also provides new adopters and any interested dog owners a list of carefully screened and approved dog training facilities and trainers. And, if the dog is determined at its first veterinary appointment to have serious and previously undetermined health problems, the owners can either return the dog for a refund or choose another dog.

As if these services weren't enough, the shelter has plans to expand on its tremendous efforts. "By the year 2000, we will be in a new facility," says Wilhite. "The new building will include a large fenced park in which people can play with their potential new pet away from the distractions of the shelter and a room specifically designed to hold obedience training and other classes, including grievance counseling."

Joint Efforts

An increasingly popular trend across the United States is to combine the county pound (with its animal control officers and veterinary technicians) with a nonprofit, private shelter. The government employees are responsible for catching and picking up strays and for euthanizing the animals. The nonprofit organization is responsible for running the adoption program. Since a nonprofit shelter is funded through the private sector, it is able to run its adoption program independently of the pound. In other words, the nonprofit organization can use its discretion in placing dogs with appropriate owners. They can pick and choose homes for the dogs. They have the authority to screen prospective owners. And they can deny an individual ownership of a dog if that person is deemed irresponsible or otherwise unfit as a dog owner.

Foster Care/Cageless Rescues

This is an interesting twist to the shelter concept. At a foster care rescue each rescued animal is kept in a person's home until the dog is adopted. What makes this type of rescue so special is that the person providing foster care for the dog knows the animal's temperament very well, along with its fears, phobias and general canine quirks.

The Animal Adoption & Rescue Foundation, Inc. (AARF) of Winston-Salem, N.C. is a foster care rescue that is run entirely by volunteers and houses approximately 50 puppies, kittens, cats and dogs at any one time. Upon being surrendered to or rescued by AARF, the animal is immediately taken to one of several veterinarians who not only gives the dog a complete veterinary exam, along with blood and stool tests, but also gives the dog a temperament evaluation. "If the veterinarian says the dog is dangerously aggressive, we take his or her word as gospel," explains Barbara Sgambellone, one of the founders of AARF. "The veterinarians we work with are extremely knowledgeable and really put these dogs through their paces. If a vet tells us that a dog is borderline and suggests we work with it a bit and see how it does, then we place the dog with a foster home that likes working with behavior problems."

While the dog is at the foster home, it is socialized with both humans and other animals. If the dog needs some basic obedience training, it gets it. If the dog needs special veterinary care, the foster parent makes sure the canine receives the attention it needs. If the dog will need several weeks at the foster home before it will be a placeable dog, the dog stays at the foster home. Of course, all of this takes money. Sgambellone explains that in order to keep the program running, AARF tries to pair each foster parent up with a sponsor. "We have volunteers that are interested in helping us financially, but do not have room to foster an animal at home. We also have those who have room for a dog, but cannot afford to pay all of the dog's expenses. To make the program work, we have to have both a sponsor and a foster parent for each animal." The AARF's adoption procedures are modeled after the rigorous methods used by most purebred rescue organizations. They include: A telephone interview, an application, a visit with the foster parent or a meeting at an animal adoption fair (held weekly at pet stores), possibly a home visit, delivery of the dog to the person's home (another home visit), follow-up phone calls, and a follow-up home visit.

Pet Fairs

It is becoming increasingly popular for large pet stores and national chains to hold "pet fairs."

On a regular basis, these stores invite rescue agencies to bring adoptable dogs and other animals to the store. Pounds, shelters, Greyhound rescues, and breed rescues are all frequent participants in programs such as this. In many cases, the shelter groups will actually bring pets that can be adopted immediately. Other groups, such as the Greyhound rescue and breed rescue groups, will more often bring a few dogs that you can meet and use the fair more as an educational and awareness tool.

Whether you are actually shopping or just looking, these pet fairs are wonderful experiences.

You are able to talk with experienced "dog" people, you get to meet the dogs, and the atmosphere is relaxed and inviting. In addition, the dogs at the fairs often are not as stressed as they would be "back at the ranch," so to speak. It is sometimes much easier to determine a dog's true colors in this more comfortable environment.

The best way to find out if there are regular pet fairs in your area, is simply to call the various pet stores that are nearby.

Newspaper Ads

Occasionally you will find an ad in the paper from a person trying to find a home for an adult dog. The advertiser is usually either someone who has found a stray dog or someone who can no longer care for their dog for whatever reason. When you call the individual, your first question should probably be "Why are you trying to place/sell this dog?" You may or may not get a straight answer, but at least it's a start. If you go to see the dog, you may be able to glean a lot about its background by just observing its current home life. In situations such as these, you will most likely NOT be able to return the dog (they're getting rid of it, after all!) nor will you be given a health guarantee or possibly even any shot records. Proceed with caution and be sure to take a knowledgeable dog person with you. An immediate visit to the vet would be highly recommended.

Neighbor

If you know both the neighbor and the dog really well, this can sometimes be a rather nice source for a dog. However, be forewarned that if there is a real problem with the dog, your friendship with the neighbor may evaporate pretty quickly. And be aware that as well as you know your neighbor, he or she may "fudge" a little on the facts of the dog. Additionally, the neighbor may, with no ill intentions, forget to tell you some pertinent information. This latter situation can happen quite often because many times a dog owner will overlook his or her dog's behavior or physical problems because the owner is just so used to them, he or she really doesn't notice them anymore.

Ann Plunkett, a mother of three young boys from Mechanicsburg, Pennsylvania, relates her experience with adopting "the neighbor's dog." A couple in the Plunkett's neighborhood was scheduled to move across the country and decided to take only one of their two dogs. Anne and her husband, Mike, agreed to take the larger of the two dogs, a 6-year-old Golden Retriever. As first time dog owners, the Plunketts were in for a few revelations. "We were surprised that he shed so much! We had no idea," laughs Plunkett, looking back at the experience. The family also discovered that the 100-lb dog was suffering from hip dysplasia. "We knew he had some problems. We just didn't know how extensive it was." In addition, she suspects that the retriever was actually quite a bit older than his prior owners had estimated. "They had gotten him from the pound, so they really weren't sure." The good side of the adoption, Plunkett relates, is that "Duncan came with some basic obedience. We didn't have to go through the puppy stage. I don't think I could have handled that." And, of course, "He's just a very, very good dog."

Pound and Shelter Dog Selections
On Your First Trip

Don't fall in love - First of all, do not walk into a shelter with the idea that you are going to walk out with a dog. Instead, go to the shelter with the idea of "window shopping." Take a look at what the shelter has to offer. If there isn't a canine that strikes your fancy, don't settle for second best. Wait a couple of weeks and go back. I realize this is an extremely difficult attitude to take, especially when you know that the dogs you see this week might very well be "gone" next week, but it is for the good of you and the dog!

Make a list - Wilhite suggests making a list of all the things you are looking for in a dog. "You need to have a good idea of what kind of pet you want before you come to the shelter. That way, if a long-haired dog won't fit into your lifestyle, you won't be as tempted to adopt one." She adds that it is a good idea to discuss this list with the shelter worker who is assisting you, too. "It makes our job much easier to help you find the right dog."

Take someone knowledgeable with you - A "knowledge-able" person is not your next door neighbor, your tennis doubles partner, or even your spouse or significant other. A "knowledgeable" dog person is someone who is actively and intensely involved with dogs. Veterinarians, obedience trainers, reputable breeders, purebred rescue workers are all knowledgeable dog people. They understand dogs and dog behavior. They can recognize potential fear biters, dominant aggressive sorts and other problem pups. They can also spot many potentially serious canine health problems. Likewise, they can tell you after spending time with the dog,"Yes, this seems like a really great dog."

Additionally, if you are a softhearted wimp (as most of us are!) when it comes to saying "no" to adopting a dog that you know in your heart won't work out a knowledgeable dog person can be the necessary "third party" you need to discourage you from making an impulsive decision.

Whatever you do, the best thing you can do is take someone with you!

How do you find someone to go with you? Pick up the phone and call. Barb McNinch, a professional trainer affiliated with DOGTRAIN in Wilmington, N.C., recommends people call and "ask if that individual provides this type of service. If they don't, ask them if they have a recommendation as to who does." McNinch says you can probably expect to pay the professional's hourly rate for the visit (anywhere from $15 to $40/hour), but the advice you will get is well worth the minimal expense in the long run and many professionals will discount their rates. "I think it's such a great thing for people to adopt adult dogs that I always discount my rate to help them in their search." Additionally, if the dog you choose to adopt has a few quirks or behaviors that will need modification, the professional is right there to tell you what you will need to do to work through these "problems."

If you choose to have a member of a breed rescue help you in your decision, the individual probably won't charge anything for their services BUT please make a generous donation to their rescue!

Check Background information - Some shelters will put temperament cards on each dog's kennel describing the dog's behavior according to the previous owner. Strays obviously don't have these cards. Always read these cards! But, keep in mind that many times an owner will lie.

And, according to Wilhite, owners amazingly don't distort the truth to improve his or her dog's chances of being placed--rather, the owner will lie in order to justify giving the dog up for adoption. "Many times owners will come in and say the dog is not housebroken or is aggressive and it's not," says Wilhite, a bit exasperated. "They've given up on the dog and they will write down almost anything to make themselves feel better."

If the shelter doesn't have information cards on the dogs' kennels, ask if the shelter requires previous owners to fill out a questionnaire when they surrendered their pet. If the answer is yes, ask to see this sheet. If, for confidentiality purposes, you are not allowed to see the sheet, ask if a shelter worker can relate to you the pertinent information about the dog.

Get advice from volunteers & shelter workers - It is always important to ask an experienced shelter worker or volunteer to give you their evaluation of the dog that you are interested in.

This, of course, can be difficult and the quality of information you will receive may vary greatly.

Some volunteers and employees are very knowledgeable and helpful. They've spent time with the dogs, played with them and walked them outside of the shelter. They understand dogs and dog behavior. These people have really taken the time to try to evaluate each dog's temperament and can be a valuable source of information. Then, on the other hand, there are those workers and volunteers who profess to be "dog experts," but really aren't. (Like the volunteer that told one woman that all Chow Chows were just great with children. "Cinnamon" proceeded to viciously attack the woman's young daughter. The dog was returned and, presumably, euthanized.)

So, how do you know if the person you are dealing with is a help or a hindrance? One way is to take an experienced dog person (veterinarian, trainer, breeder, breed rescue worker, etc.) with you and let them ask the questions. Another way is just to ask an awful lot of questions. Work on your list of questions, in advance!

You'll want to know how the dog reacts when it is being fed, when its food is taken away, how it responds to being handled, and how it reacts to men, to women, to people with disabilities (some dogs are frightened by an awkward walk or sporadic movements). Find out if the dog soils its kennel often and then ask how frequently the dogs are allowed "run"time to relieve themselves.

Ask if the dog has shown any unusual responses to anything - brushes, pooper scoopers, hoses, whatever. Does the dog have any phobias? Is it frightened easily? Is it shy? Is it aggressive toward other dogs? How long has it been at the shelter? How did it arrive there? All of these questions and more can help you piece together a dog's past and potential temperament. Don't be shy!

Make Time to Play - If you think you've found a dog you like, ask the shelter workers if you can take the dog to a private area to spend some time with it. Some shelters have an outdoor area where you spend quality time with the dog. Others do not. If the shelter does not have a private fenced area to work with the dog for a little bit, ask if you can take the dog for a walk. Be sure to bring a leash.

When you are with the dog, you'll want to observe several things. (Did you bring your dog expert with you?) Start slowly with the dog. Speak gently to it. Does it respond to a pleasant voice? Does it want attention and pats? Throw a ball and play some games with the dog. Does the dog allow you to take the ball out of its mouth? If you've brought treats, does the dog take them gently from your hand?

As you become more familiar with the dog, pet it over its entire body. Be careful! If the dog has a tender area (as some gun shot or otherwise wounded dogs do have), a prod in the wrong place might elicit a bite. Pick up the dog's paws - will it allow you to clip its nails? If you feel pretty confident with the dog, see if you can check its ears, eyes, and finally its teeth. Can you gently hug the dog?

After having handled and played with the dog for a while, observe if it has settled down. Many dogs get stressed in a kennel situation and can be quite hyper when first taken into a play area. A truly hyper dog will not settle down very much. An active dog will be excited, but should calm down somewhat after a period of time.

The longer time period you can spend with the dog, the better you will be able to judge the dog's temperament. However, even a dog expert will admit that at best, this is an educated guess. A shelter is really not the same as meeting and greeting the dog in someone's home or in another comfortable, nonthreatening atmosphere.

Indicators of Problem Dogs: An Aggression Primer

Wayne Hunthausen, D.V.M., director of Animal Behavior Consultations at Westwood Animal Hospital, and past president of the American Veterinary Society of Animal Behavior, recommends that it is wise to observe the dog's reactions to vis tors, particularly children. "A charging dog is dangerous and should not be adopted," says Hunthausen. "Likewise, if the dog is on a leash and is lunging aggressively at people or your own children, that's unacceptable, too."

Of course, these exhibitions of aggression are fairly obvious. What many people do not realize is that there are several other more subtle forms of aggression that can be equally as dangerous.

Fear Aggression - This form of aggression is one of the most common reasons for dog bite injuries to people. And, unfortunately, children are prime targets because they often don't realize that you can't comfort a frightened dog in the same way that a mother comforts a child. In other words, a frightened dog does not respond well to hugs.

Indicators of fear are ears that are low to the head, cowering, tail between the legs, freezing in place, shaking or leaning away from people. Unless you're looking for trouble, it is advisable to stay away from a fearful or shy animal.

Dominant aggression - This form of aggression can be very subtle and difficult to detect at first.

A dominant aggressive dog tries to maintain an "alpha" or top dog ranking in its canine and human packs. Other pets, young children and adults may be "bossed" around or even injured by dogs that are dominant aggressive. Before any problems occur, Hunthausen recommends getting the pet into obedience classes right away and reviewing the commands and methods used with all family members. "You can even hold a young child in your lap and the two of you give the dog a sit command. When the dog obeys, have the child reward the dog by tossing it a treat. In this way, the child is taking control over the dog."

Possessive aggression - In this form of aggression, a dog is possessive with what it perceives as its possessions. This could be the dog's food, bed, toys or other items. Many times this behavior can be modified with professional help, but much of the dog's rehabilitation depends on the dog and the extent of the aggression itself. Signs of this type of aggression are growling or snapping when you try to take a toy away or attempt to pick up the dog's food.

Territorial aggression - Territorial aggression is generally not dangerous to your immediate family, but it is risky to children "passing through" your yard. Hunthausen advises watching carefully how the dog responds to other people and animals when it is on a leash. If the dog growls, barks, or lunges, you may have to work with a professional to modify the dog's behavior.

In addition, you may have to ensure that your dog never comes in contact with trespassers. Predatory aggression - Fortunately, this lethal form of aggression is not very common. However, when it does appear, it is extremely dangerous, with small infants being in particular jeopardy. "This is a very different form of aggression," explains Hunthausen. "The dog with predatory aggression will focus at a child in the same way an ordinary dog would focus in on a squirrel. The dog will appear very alert or perform stalking behavior, holding its body low to the ground." This form of aggression is a behavior that can rarely be controlled, much less corrected. DO NOT ADOPT THIS DOG. In fact, if the dog displays this behavior, report it to the shelter workers in order that the proper action can be taken.

In general, it's just a good rule of thumb to avoid adopting dogs with any obvious signs of aggression, regardless of the source of the aggression. A dog is supposed to be a loving, loyal and trustworthy companion. It shouldn't bite the hand that feeds it! And, if you are a parent, your priorities should be with providing a safe environment for your children - rather than to attempt to rescue a troublesome and potentially dangerous canine.

Not judging all books by their covers - Of course, judging what is a form of aggression and what is actually a breed's unique response to being in a shelter situation is a very fine line to walk and probably is best left to those who know best. It is interesting to note, however, that shelter situations really do bring out the worst (and sometimes temporary) behaviors in some breeds. Catherine Romaine Brown, humane officer of the Jack Russell Terrier Club of America "Russell Rescue" and author of The Jack Russell Terrier: An Owner's Guide to a Happy, Healthy Pet (Howell Book House: 1996), says that Jack Russell Terriers are many times passed over in shelters because of their response to their surroundings. "The reactions we see most often are that of either cowering in the corner of their cage or behavior similar to a raging maniac, neither of which appears very adoptable," admits Brown. "However, if you are allowed to take the dog for a walk away from the shelter, you'll most likely see an immediate transformation. It's like, 'Phew! Someone finally got me out of there!' By the end of the walk, you'll know whether you have a friend on the end of the leash or not."

McNinch warns that guard dogs such as Rotties may also give the impression of being an undesirable or volatile dog at the shelter. "The Rottweiler is very loyal to the person it respects as its owner. When you walk into the shelter, you are not its owner and you don't have its respect - yet," explains McNinch. "If you make direct eye contact with the dog, it may very well see you as something it should guard against. That's why I always make it a point to avert my eye contact when initially meeting the dog." McNinch adds that once a person is able to establish leadership with the dog, many times the dog will eagerly and willingly transfer its loyalty to the new, adoptive owner.

You can probably see by now just how tricky it is to evaluate a dog's temperament in a shelter situation. You certainly don't want to overlook a perfectly loveable dog because it is overwhelmed by the shelter and is displaying odd behavior; on the other hand, you absolutely don't want to make a disastrous mistake by adopting the canine equivalent of Freddy Krueger.

This is why I keep harping for prospective adopters to take a dog expert with them to the shelter!

Bring everyone - If this dog is to be a family dog, bring your family. Grandparents, spouses, teenagers, and youngsters should all have a chance to meet the dog before an adoption takes place. Carefully watch the interaction between your family members and the dog. (See Dogs & Kids.) If you have small children, this is critically important.

Take notes - As you visit shelters and play with dogs, take notes after each dog and/or visit. It is very easy to quickly forget negative attributes and remember only the positive ones. Also, if you have any apprehensions or questions, note these, too. If there is no one at the shelter who can answer your questions, and you did not bring a dog buddy (for shame!), you'll want to have these questions handy to ask your veterinarian or dog aficionado at a later time.

Mull it over - If you think you've found the perfect dog, make a hold deposit (if the shelter allows this) on the animal and then go home. Give yourself at least 24-hours to think it over. If in the morning, you are still as excited as ever about this canine, you can make a second visit to the shelter and begin the adoption process.

The Adoption Process

Once you've found the dog of your dreams which, of course, is not aggressive or fearful, you are ready to do some paperwork.

Screening/Application

Many of the better staffed and well-funded shelters are able to provide screening services in which the prospective dog owner is required to fill out an application and be interviewed by someone at the shelter. The questions on the application and the interview process will be very similar to what has previously been outlined in the breed rescue chapter. As always, be honest!

And, if the shelter has some suggestions as to how you can better your situation for responsible dog ownership, be open to suggestions.

> **The contract** - Depending on the shelter and their policies, you can expect to sign a contract that holds the shelter harmless of any damages or injuries your new dog might cause. The contract will most likely include a spay/neuter requirement.

> **Return policies** - Before you sign on the dotted line, be sure to ask the shelter what their policies are on dogs with severe health problems. For instance, if you take the dog to have its vet exam and discover that it has such a severe infestation of heartworm that the vet recommends that the dog be euthanized, what will the shelter do? Will they return your adoption fee or allow you to pick out another dog at no cost? Will they take the dog back (and euthanize it themselves)? Be sure to ask. Also, don't be shy about asking what the shelter's general return policy is. If the dog turns out to be a dominant aggressive sort and is trying to push your kindergartner around, can you return the dog and choose another canine? Or will the shelter make you pay a surrender fee and another adoption fee?

> **Discounted services** - Many veterinarians, groomers and pet supply stores try to support adult dog adoption and offer discounts to new dog adopters. Ask the shelter if they have any

such agreements with local merchants or if there are any non-profit organizations in the area that help subsidize such things as spay/neuters. You might be in for a pleasant surprise! It never hurts to ask.

Follow-up assistance - Some of the better organized (and funded) shelters offer adoptive owners everything from discounted obedience training classes and basic pet care counseling to 24-hour "help" hotlines. Obedience classes and pet care counseling are particularly important to the new dog owner. If the shelter doesn't offer any such things, ask the director who does. The shelter should be able to provide you with a list of local obedience clubs and ongoing class schedules. If not, your veterinarian is always a terrific source of information and behavioral counseling.

Never say never - Rarely is there a behavioral problem that can't be corrected with a little time, patience, and the correct modification training. When you adopt an adult dog from a shelter, remember that the same problems that existed before the dog came to the shelter are now your problems. The difference is that you are willing to work with your dog and make him into a model canine citizen. So, never say that your dog will never be a member of the family - it will.

You've just got to be committed to making the situation work - and you've got to ask the right people the right questions. If you are having problems, don't be shy about calling the shelter, your veterinarian, a breeder, or a rescue worker for some advice. As dog lovers, these people would much rather answer what you fear are endless questions than see another happy, healthy dog end up a canine statistic.

Appendix A: Sources for Adult Purebread Dogs National Breed Clubs, Breeder Referral Contacts and Breed Rescues

AKC Registered Breeds: All national breed clubs belonging to the AKC have secretaries, and most have breeder referral contacts and national breed rescue chairpersons. Secretaries and correspondance secretaries are responsible for distributing breed information and are also a wealth of information in general. If no one is listed as a "breeder referral" or breed rescue contact for the breed you are interested in, ask the club secretary who you can contact.

All information was current at the time of printing, however, names, numbers and addresses do change. If the name or number is not current for the breed you are interested in, call the AKC's consumer information for an updated listing.

Non-AKC Registered/Rare Breeds: Rare and unusual breeds need rescuing, too! If the rare breed your are looking for is not listed in this appendix, call the American Rare Breed Association or the United Kennel Club. The Internet is also a good search start, too.

Registries

American Kennel Club: 5580 Centerview Dr., Raleigh, NC 27606 (919) 233-9767; www.akc.org

American Rare Breed Association: P.O. Box 76424, Washington, DC 20013 (202) 722-1232

United Kennel Club: 100 East Kilgore Rd., Kalamazoo, MI 49001-5598 (616) 343-9020

AKC - Sporting Group

American Brittany Club, Inc.
Corres. Secretary: Joy Searcy, 800 Hillmont Ranch Rd., Aldeo, TX 76008
Breeder Referral Contact: Ms. Velma Tiedeman, 2036 N. 48th Ave.,
Omaha, NE 68104 (402) 553-5538
Breed Rescue: Rhonda Carlson (510) 582-2714 (home);
(510) 549-2527 (work); CA

American Pointer Club, Inc.
Secretary: Henri B. Tuthill, 20325 Magnolia Ave., Nuevo, CA 92567
Breed Rescue: Nancy Tuthill 1-800-807-POINT; CA

German Shorthaired Pointer Club of America
Secretary: Mary Beth Kirkland, 9702 Gayton Rd., #309, Richmond, VA
23233-4907
Breeder Referral Contact: Ann King, 11946 NYS Rt. #34N, Cato, NY
13033 (315) 626-2990
Breed Rescue: Nancy Campbell (203) 938-8048 (CT);
Bonnie Wilcox, DVM (309) 534-8112 (IL)

German Wirehaired Pointer Club of America, Inc.
Corres. Secretary: Karen Nelsen, 25821 Lucille Ave., Lomita, CA 90717
Breeder Referral Contact: Mrs. Nancy Mason, 826 Cinebar Rd., Cinebar,
WA 98533 (360) 985-2776
Breed Rescue: Linda Strothman (508) 249-8360 (MA)

American Chesapeake Club, Inc.
Corres. Secretary: Nancy Boylan, 619 14th Place, Kenosha, WI 53140
Breeder Referral Contact: American Chesapeake Club, P.O. Box 523,
Florissant, MO 63032-0523 (314) 653-1718
Breed Rescue: None

Curly-Coated Retriever Club of America
Corres. Secretary: Penny A.W. Sleeth, 16594 You Bet Road, Grass Valley,
CA 95945-8662
Breeder Referral Contact: Same as above
Breed Rescue: Shella Callahan-Young (508) 281-3860 (MA)

Flat-Coated Retriever Society of America, Inc.
Corres Secretary, Miriam Krum, 16705 W. 327th St., Paola, KS 66071
Breeder Referral Contact: Same as above (913) 849-3218
Breed Rescue: Joyce Rein (616) 846-0773 (MI)

Golden Retriever Club of America
Secretary: Linda Willard, 10604, Spring Valley, Austin, TX 78736
Breeder Referral Contact: Linda Willard, 9900 Broadway, Suite 102,
Oklahoma City, OK 73114 (512) 301-3499
Breed Rescue: Tom Congleton (602) 596-9293 (AZ)

Labrador Retriever Club, Inc.
Secretary: 12471 Pond Road, Burton, OH 44021;
E-mail: Rodarbal@aol.com
Breeder Referral Contact: None
Breed Rescue: Luanne Lindsey (512) 259-3625 (TX)

English Setter Association of America, Inc.
Secretary: Mrs. Dawn S. Ronyak, 114 S. Burlington Oval Dr., Chardon,
OH 44024
Breeder Referral Contact: Same as above (216) 285-4531
Breed Rescue: Cheryl Minnier (417) 928-7936 (MO)

Gordon Setter Club of America, Inc.
Corres. Secretary: Nikki Maounis, P.O. Box 54, Washougal, WA 98671
Breeder Referral Contact: Ms. Phyllis Tew, 7707 S. Rosemary Way,
Englewood, CO 80112 (303) 841-2015
Breed Rescue: Crystal Todor (614) 879-8405 (OH)

Irish Setter Club of America, Inc.
Corres. Secretary: Mrs. Marion Pahy, 16717 Ledge Falls, San Antonio,
TX 78232-1808
Breeder Referral Contact: Mrs. Marilee Larson, 27371 Whitmor, Pioneer,
CA 95666 (209) 295-1666
Breed Rescue: Mrs. Marilee Larson (Info above)

American Water Spaniel Club
Secretary: Patricia A. St. Onge, 4835 S. Mill Loop Rd., Maple, WI
54854-9011
Breeder Referral Contact: Madie Kolk, 16542 James St., Holland, MI
49424 1-800-555-2972
Breed Rescue: Marie Kangas (612) 434-9373 (MN)

Clumber Spaniel Club of America, Inc.
Secretary: Ms. Barbara Stebbins, 2271 SW Almansa Ave., Port St. Lucie, FL 34953
Breeder Referral Contact: Edythe Donovan, 241 Monterey Ave., Pelham, NY 10801 (914) 738-3976
Breed Rescue: Sue Carr (908) 580-1055 (NJ)

American Spaniel Club, Inc.
Corres. Secretary: Margaret M. Ciezkowski, 846 Old Stevens Creed Rd., Martinez, GA 30907-9227
Breeder Referral Contact: Dorothy Mustard, 30 Cardinal Loop, Crossville, TN 38555 (615) 484-5434
Breed Rescue: None

English Cocker Spaniel Club of America, Inc.
Secretary: Kate D. Romanski, P.O. Box 252, Hales Corners, WI 53130
Breeder Referral Contact: Same as above (414) 529-9714
Breed Rescue: Dr. Marsha Wallace (703) 548-7641 (VA)

Field Spaniel Society of America
Corres. Secretary: Becki Jo Wolkenheim, P.O. Box 187, Wales, WI 53183
Breeder Referral Contact: Sharon Douthit, 1905 Ave. J., Sterling, IL 61081 (815) 625-0467
Breed Rescue: Pat Ramsey (714) 761-7144 (CA)

Irish Water Spaniel Club of America
Secretary: Renae Peterson, 24712 SE 380th St., Enumelaw, WA 98022-8833
Breeder Referral Contact: Same as above (360) 825-6128
Breed Rescue: Carolyn Lathrop (301) 724-9162 (MD)

Sussex Spaniel Club of America
Corres. Secretary: Sue Caniff, 2435 E. Aldine, Phoenix, AZ 85032
Breeder Referral Contact: Ms. Kathy Miller, 422 Ward Ave., Girard, OH 44420 (330) 545-6996
Breed Rescue: None

Welsh Springer Spaniel Club of America, Inc.
Corres.Secretary: Karen Lyle, 4425 N. 147th St., Brookfield, WI 53005-1608
Breeder Referral Contact: Pat Pencak, 135 Old Forrestburg Rd., Sparrow Bush, NY 12780 (914)856-4533
Breed Rescue: Peggy Ruble (316) 244-3782 (KS)

Viszla Club of America, Inc.
Corres. Secretary: Mrs. Florence Duggan, 452 Longfellow Ave., Westfield, NJ 07090
Breeder Referral Contact: Same as above (908) 789-9774
Breed Rescue: Luellen Hart (501) 888-7333 (AZ)

Weimaraner Club of America
Corres. Secretary: Marge Davis, 13188 Flamingo Terr., Lake Park, FL 33410
Breeder Referral Contact: Ms. Rebecca Weimer, 324 Sundew Dr., Belleville, IL 62221 (618)236-1466
Breed Rescue: Ms. Rebecca Weimer (Info listed above)

AKC - Hound Group

Afghan Hound Club of America
Corres. Secretary, Norma Cozzoni, 43 W. 612 Tall Oaks Trail, Elburn, IL 60119
Breeder Referral Contact: Same as above. (708) 365-3647
Breed Rescue: Judy Fellton (404) 971-1533 (GA)

Basenji Club of America
Secretary: Anne L. Graves, 5102 Darnell, Houston, TX 77096-1404
Breeder Referral Contact: Melody Russell, 2714 NE 110th St., Seattle, WA 98125 (206) 362-4202

Breed Rescue: Judith Holiday (303) 795-5382 (CO)
Basset Hound Club of America, Inc.
Secretary: Melody Fair, P.O. Box 339, Noti, OR 97461
Breeder Referral Contact: Mrs. Ruth Balladone, 15818 Highland Circle, Redding, CA 96001 (916) 244-3403
Breed Rescue: Libby Sallada (B.H. Cares) (303) 798-0942 (CO.)

National Beagle Club
Secretary: Susan Mills Stone, 2555 Pennsylvania NW, Washington, DC 20037
Breeder Referral Contact: Nadine Cuicoine, P.O. Box 1710, Leonardtown, MD 20650
Breed Rescue: None

American Black & Tan Coonhound
Secretary: Stan Bielowicz, 7222 Pate Rogers Rd., Fleming, GA 31309
Breeder Referral Contact: Cheryl Speed, 3508 Berger Rd., Lutz, FL
33549 (813) 963-2033
Breed Rescue: Chris Hooker (919) 776-7375 (NC)

American Bloodhound Club
Secretary: Ed Kilby, 1914 Berry Lane, Daytona Beach, FL 32124
Breeder Referral Contact: Same as above (904) 788-0137
Breed Rescue: Same as above

Borzoi Club of America, Inc.
Corres. Secretary: Karen Mays, 29 Crown Dr., Warren, NJ 07059-5111
Breeder Referral Contact: Same as above (908) 647-3027
Breed Rescue: Barbara Skinner (908) 859-4554 (NJ)

Dachshund Club of America, Inc.
Secretary: Mr. Walter M. Jones, 390 Eminence Pike, Shelbyville, KY
40065
Breeder Referral Contact: Mrs. Dorothy Hutchinson, East Woods, Rd.,
Pound Ridge, NY 10576 (914) 764-5226
Breed Rescue: Emma Jean Stephenson (412) 846-6745 (PA)

Greyhound Club of America (This is the AKC club - NOT retired track dogs)
Corres. Secretary: Margaret Bryson, 15079 Meeting House Lane,
Montpelier, VA 23292
Breeder Referral Contact: Same as above (804) 883-7800
Breed Rescue (AKC dogs only): Cheryl Reynolds (805) 684-4914 (CA)

Harrier Club of America
Secretary: Kimberly Mitchell, 301 Jefferson Lane, Ukiah, CA 95482
Breeder Referral Contact: Same as above (707) 463-0501
Breed Rescue: None

Ibizan Hound Club of the United States
Secretary: Jeffrey Macek, 2536 E. Whitton Ave., Phoeniz, AZ 85016-7422
Breeder Referral Contact: Lisa Puskas, 4312 E. Nisbet Rd., Phoenix, AZ
85032 (602) 493-7080
Breed Rescue: Lisa Puskas (Information listed above)

Irish Wolfhound Club of America
Secretary: Mrs. William S. Pfarrer, 8855 U.S. Route 40, New Carlisle, OH 45344
Breeder Referral Contact: Same as above (513) 845-9135
Breed Rescue: Jean A Minnier (609) 268-9373 (NJ)

Norwegian Elkhound Association of America, Inc.
Corres. Secretary: Debra Walker, 3650 Bay Creek Rd., Loganville, GA 30249
Breeder Referral Contact: Same as above (770) 466-9967
Breed Rescue: Lois Mills (517) 871-3284 (MI)

Otterhound Club of America
Corres. Secretary: Dian Quist-Sulek, Rt. #1, Box 247, Palmyra, NE 68418
Breeder Referral Contact: Same as above. (412) 799-3535
Breed Rescue: Betsy Conway (914) 245-6354 (NY)

Petit Basset Griffon Vendeen Club of America
Secretary: Ms. Shirley Knipe, 426 Laguna Way, Simi Valley, CA 93065
Breeder Referral Contact: Same as above. (805) 527-6327
Breed Rescue: Debbie Perrott (805) 527-6327 (CA)

Pharoah Hound Club of America
Corres. Secretary: Rita L. Sacks, P.O. Box 895454, Leesburg, FL 34789-5454
Breeder Referral Contact: Same as above (352) 357-8723
Breed Rescue: Libby Leone (408) 663-2550 (CA)

Rhodesian Ridgeback Club of the United States, Inc.
Corres. Secretary: Betty J. Epperson, P.O. Box 121817, Ft. Worth, TX 76121-1817
Breeder Referral Contact: Jacque Rex, 25198 E. 19th St., San Bernardino, CA 92404 (909) 381-3064
Breed Rescue: Dana Jefferson (302) 454-7598 (DE)

Saluki Club of America
Secretary: Donna J. Kappmeier, 12192 Gilbert St., Garden Grove, CA 92641
Breeder Referral Contact: Ms. Cloris Costigan, 7 Huntington Rd., East Brunswick, NJ 08816 (980) 257-9134
Breed Rescue: Cloris Costigan (908) 257-9134 (N.J.)

Scottish Deerhound Club of America, Inc.
Secretary: Mrs. Joan Shagan, 545 Cummings Lane, Cottontown, TN 37048
Breeder Referral Contact: Ms. Bette Stencil, 1328 S. Riverside Ave., St. Claire, MI 48079-5133 (810) 329-3841
Breed Rescue: Deborah Day Hughes (517) 769-2444 (MI)

American Whippet Club, Inc.
Secretary: Mrs. Harriet Nash Lee, 14 Oak Circle, Charlottesville, VA 22901
Breeder Referral Contact: Same as above. (804) 295-4525
Breed Rescue: Sally DeBecque Smith (303) 666-9614 (CO)

AKC - Working Group

Akita Club of America
Secretary: Anne Marie Taylor, 8083 Turner Rd., Fenton, MI 48430
Breeder Referral Contact: Mrs. Debbie Steward, 17945 Jo Ann Way, Perris, CA 92570-8961 (909) 943-1811
Breed Rescue: Nancy Baun (201) 427-5985 (N.J.)

Alaskan Malamute Club of America, Inc.
Corres. Secretary: Stephen Piper, 3528 Pin Hook Road, Antioch, TN 37013-1510
Breeder Referral Contact: Cap Schneider, 21 Unneberg Ave., Succasunna, NJ 07876 (201) 584-7125
Breed Rescue: Virginia A. Devaney (505) 281-3961 (NM)

Bernese Moutain Dog Club of America, Inc.
Secretary: Ms. Roxanne Bortnick, P.O. Box 270692, Fort Collins, Co 80527
Breeder Referral Contact: Ms. Ruth Reynold, 5265 E. Fort Rd., Greenwood, FL 32443 (904) 594-4636
Breed Rescue: Beth Friichtenicht, (309) 596-2633 (IL)

American Boxer Club, Inc.
Corres. Secretary: Mrs. Barbara E. Wagner, 6310 Edward Dr., Clinton, MD 20735-4135
Breeder Referral Contact: Mrs. Lucille Jackson, 11300 Oakton Rd., Oakton, VA 22124 (703) 385-9385
Breed Rescue: Tracy Hendrickson (918) 665-1767 (work); (918) 250-

9004 (home); (OK)
American Bullmastiff Association, Inc.
Secretary: Ms. MaryAnne Duchin, P.O. Box 37, Dayton, KY 41074
Breeder Referral Contact: Ms. Barbara Brooks-Warrell, 16045 SE 196th,
Kent, WA 98042; E-mail: bbrooks@u.washington.edu
Breed Rescue: Ms. Barbara Brooks-Worrell (206) 850-6319 (WA)

Doberman Pinscher Club of America
Corres. Secretary: Mrs. Tommie F. Jones, 4840 Thomasville Rd.,
Tallahassee, FL 32308
Breeder Contact: Same as above (904) 668-1735
Breed Rescue: Judith S. Felton (404) 971-1533 (GA)

Giant Schnauzer Club of America, Inc.
Secretary: Robin Greenslade, 12 Walnut Terrace, Salem, NH 03079
Breeder Referral Contact: Same as above (603) 894-4938
Breed Rescue: Carolyn Janak (303) 988-6564

Great Dane Club of America, Inc.
Corres. Secretary: Kathy Jurin, 1825 Oaklyn Dr., Green Lane, PA 18054
Breeder Referral Contact: "Pookie" Kostuk, P.O. Box 2015, Cheshire, CT
06410 (203) 272-8292
Breed Rescue: Eleanor Evans (619) 722-1037 (CA); Erin McGlynn
(The Great Dane Club of Western Pennyslvania) (412) 361-2968,
E-mail: Pennsylvania Erinm@pitt.edu

Great Pyrenees Club of America, Inc.
Corres. Secretary: Maureen Maxwell-Simon, 7430 Jonestown,
Harrisburg, PA 17112
Breeder Referral Contact: Janet Ingram, 204 Wild Partridge Lane,
Radford, VA 24141 (540) 731-0299; E-mail: jlingram@nrv.net
Breed Rescue: Janet Ingram (Information listed above)

Komondor Club of America, Inc.
Corres. Secretary: Ms Sandra Hanson, W359, S10708 Nature Rd., Eagle
WI 53119
Breeder Referral Contact: Same as above (414) 594-3374
Breed Rescue: Same as above

Greater Swiss Mountain Dog Club of America, Inc.
Corres. Secretary: De Anne Gerner, 91 Shoffers Rd., Reading, PA 19606
Breeder Referral Contact: None
Breed Rescue: DeAnne Gerner (610) 779-9217 (Pa.); Sharyl Mayhew
(703) 754-0158 (Va.); Kathy Caslin (309) 334-2883 (IL)

Kuvasz Club of America
Corres. Secretary: Jody Tillotson, 3240 Richards Dr., Snellville, GA 30278
Breeder Referral Contact: Pat Zupan, 2706 Garfield St., Township, N.J.
07719 (908) 681-3096
Breed Rescue: Mayling Koval (919) 562-0610 (NC)

Mastiff Club of America, Inc.
Corres. Secretary: Karen McBee, Rt. #7, Box 520, Fairmont, WV 26554;
E-mail: mmcbee@access.mountain.net
Breeder Referral Contact: Ms. Carla Sanchez, 45935 Via Esperanza,
Temecula, CA 92590 (203) 966-4253
Breed Rescue: Paula Lange (602) 476-4605 (AZ)

Newfoundland Club of America, Inc.
Corres. Secretary: Sandee Lovett, 5870 5 Mile Rd., NE, Ada, MI 49301
Breeder Referral Contact: Rebecca Cieniewicz, 341 Carter's Gin Rd.,
Toney, AL 35773 (205) 852-7015
Breed Rescue: Mary L. Price (608) 437-4553 (WI)

Portuguese Water Dog Club of America, Inc.
Corres. Secretary: Cheryl G. Smith, 116 Teresita Way, Los Gatos, CA
95032; E-mail: desmith@best.com
Breeder Referral Contact: Arlene Gordon, 5051 E. Orchid Lane,
Paradise Valley, AZ 85253 (602) 948-0118;
E-mail: wilgord@paloverde.com
Breed Rescue: Mary Harkins (215) 257-9570 (PA)

American Rottweiler Club
Corres. Secretary: doreen LePage, 960 S. Main St., Pascoag, RI 02859;
E-mail: doreen@ids.net
Breeder Referral Contact: Lauri Ladwig, 1184 E. Fleetwood Ct., Boise,
ID 83706 (208) 384-9881

Breed Rescue: Sandy Gilbert (217) 222-5541 (IL)
St. Bernard Club of America, Inc.
Corres. Secretary: Cheryl Zappala, 1043 S. 140th, Seattle WA 98168
Breeder Referral Contact: Same as above (206) 242-7480
Breed Rescue: Carol Varner Beck (541) 878-8281 (OR)

Samoyed Club of America, Inc.
Corres. Secretary: Sandy Hill, 4582 NE Sunnyview Rd., Salem, OR 97305-1872 (503) 363-2897
Breeder Referral Contact: Same as above
Breed Rescue: Gail Spieker (415) 325-8115 (CA)

Siberian Husky Club of America, Inc.
Corres. Secretary: Mrs. Fain B. Zimmerman, 65 Madera Dr., Victoria, TX 77905-4847
Breeder Referral Contact: Ms. Sandra Jessop, 152 Hemstead Ave., Malverne, NY 11565 (516)887-7189
Breed Rescue: Gerry Dalakian (908) 782-2089 (NJ)

Standard Schnauzer Club of America
Secretary: Lis Hansen, P.O. Box 153, Kampsvill, IL 62053
Breeder Referral Contact: Darlene Cornell, P.O. Box 87, Wappinger Falls, NY 12590 (914) 838-9207
Breed Rescue: Linda Briesacher (314) 271-2321 (MO)

AKC - Terrier Group

Airedale Terrier Club of America
Corres. Secretary: Dr. Suzanne Hampton, 47 Tulip Ave., Ringwood, NJ 07456
Breeder Referral Contact: Corally Burmaster, RR 1, Box 349E, Leesburg, VA 22075 (703) 779-8030
Breed Rescue: Barbara Curtiss (860) 927-3420 New England; Lou Swafford (301) 572-7116
Mid-Atlantic; Linda Baake (919) 726-7703 South; Carol Domeracki (616) 276-6390 Midwest; Melissa Moore (602) 996-9648 West; Connie Turner (503) 399-9819 Northwest

Breed Rescue: Jacolyn Moss (616) 847-0275 (MI)
American Fox Terrier Club
Secretary: Mr. Martin Goldstein, P.O. Box 604, South Plainfield, NJ 07080-0604
Breeder Referral Contact: Same as above. (908) 668-0715
Breed Rescue: Pam Bishop 1-888-FOX-TERR (CA)

Irish Terrier Club of America
Corres. Secretary: Cora Rivera, 22720 Perry St., Perris, CA 92570
Breeder Referral Contact: Jeanne Burrage, 103 N. Frazier Ave., Florence, CO 81226 (719) 784-0931
Breed Rescue: James Cassidy (818) 366-6233 (CA)

United States Kerry Blue Terrier Club, Inc.
Corres. Secretary: Mrs. Walter Fleisher, 443 Buena Vista Rd., New City, NY 10956
Breeder Referral Contact: Lisa Frankland 690 Korina St., Vandenberg AFB, CA 93437 (805) 734-1280; E-mail: lisaf@seldon.terminus.com
Breed Rescue: Joanne Schindler (513) 742-3745 (OH)

United States Lakeland Terrier Club
Secretary: Mrs. Edna Lawicki, 8207 E. Cholla St., Scottsdale, AZ 85260
Breeder Referral Contact: Same as above. (602) 998-8409
Breed Rescue: Mrs. Sandra Beatson (404) 513-7431 (GA)

American Manchester Terrier Club
Secretary: Sandra Kipp, 5244 Rottinghaus Rd., Rt 7, Waterloo, IA 50701
Breeder Referral Contact: Ms. Diana Haywood, 52 Hampton Rd., Pittstown, NJ 08867 (908) 996-7309
Breed Rescue: Patricia Hall 9215) 957-0109 (PA)

Miniature Bull Terrier Club of America
Corres. Secretary: Kathy Bronson, P.O. Box 634, Kingston, NH 03848
Breeder Referral Contact: Susan Hall, 5641 Mount Gilead Rd., Centreville, VA 22020 (703) 631-3565
Breed Rescue: Kathy Bronson (603) 642-5355 (NH)

American Miniature Schnauzer Club, Inc.
Secretary: Mrs. Susan R. Atherton, RR2, Box 3570, Bartlesville, OK 74003
Breeder Referral Contact: Amy Gordon, 3749 Victoria Dr., W. Palm Beach, FL 33406 (407) 964-4497

Staffordshire Terrier Club of America
Secretary: Mr. H. Richard Pascoe, 785 Valley View Rd., Forney, TX 75126
Breeder Referral Contact: None
Breed Rescue: None

Australian Terrier Club of America, Inc.
Corres. Secretary: Ms. Marilyn Harban, 1515 Davon Ln., Nassaue Bay, TX 77058
Breeder Referral Contact: Mrs. Barbara Deer, 1868 Hovsons Blvd., Toms River, NJ 08753 (908) 255-7594
Breed Rescue:Barbara Curtis (970) 482-9163 (CO)

Bedlington Terrier Club of America
Corres. Secretary: Mr. Robert Bull, P.O. Box 11, Morrison, IL 61270-7419
Breeder Referral Contact: Same as above (815) 772-4832
Breed Rescue: Ruth Mary Schneider (804) 232-3748 (VA)

Border Terrier Club of America, Inc.
Secretary: Pattie Pfeffer, 801 Los luceros Dr., Eagle, ID 83616
Breeder Referral Contact: Judy Donaldson, 135 Westledge Rd., W. Simsbury, CT 06092 (203) 651-0140
Breed Rescue: Jo Ellen Wolf (706) 863-0951 (GA)

Bull Terrier Club of America
Corres. Secretary: Mrs. Becky Poole, 2630 Gold Point Circle, Hixson, TN 37343
Breeder Referral Contact: Same as above (615) 842-2611
Breed Rescue: Norma Shepherd 1-800-BTBT-911; (401) 231-0979 (RI)

Cairn Terrier Club of America
Corres. Secretary: Christine M. Bowlus, 8096 Chilson Rd., Pinckney, MI 48169
Breeder Referral Contact: Same as above. (810) 231-4147
Breed Rescue: Betty Marcum (817) 783-5979 (Texas); Karen Smith (619) 728-7133 (CA); Susan DeWitt (203) 846-3345 (CT)

Dandie Dinmont Terrier Club of America, Inc.
Secretary: Mrs. Gail Isner, 151 Junaluska Dr., Woodstock, GA 30188
Breeder Referral Contact: Mrs. Lloyd Brewer, 1016 Mars Dr., Colorado Springs, CO 80906 (719) 473-9560

Breed Rescue: Joyce K. Somero (810) 656-4132 (MI)
Norwich and Norfolk Terrier Club
Corres. Secretary: Heidi H. Evans, 158 Delaware Ave., Laurel, DE 19956
Breeder Referral Contact: Mrs. Susan Ely, 85 Mountain Top Rd.,
Bernardsville, NJ 07924   (908) 766-3468
Breed Rescue: Susan Ely (Information above)

Scottish Terrier Club of America
Corres.Secretary:Evelyn D. Kirk, 2603 Derwnet Dr. SW, Roanoke, VA 24015
Breeder Referral Contact: Same as above. (703) 345-2998
Breed Rescue: William Berry (201) 227-1871 (NJ)

American Sealyham Terrier Club
Secretary: Judy E. Thill, 13948 N. Cascade Rd., Dubuque, IA 52003
Breeder Referral Contact: Mrs. Patsy Underwood, 3206 W. Cortez Ct.,
Irving, TX 75062 (214) 255-3581
Breed Rescue: Barbra Carmany (216) 239-1498 (OH)

Skye Terrier Club of America
Secretary: Ms. Maida Connor, 7 Fox Hill Avenue, Bristol, RI 02809
Breeder Referral Contact: Donna C. Dale, 180 March Creek Road,
Gettysburg, PA 17325 (717) 334-0303; E-mail: daleb@pa.net
Breed Rescue: Ann Brown (803) 726-3237 (home) (SC)

Soft Coated Wheaton Terrier Club of America
Corres. Secretary: John Giles, 15805 Honolulu, Houston, TX 77040
Breeder Referral Contact: Mrs. Elaine Nerrie, 1945 Edgewood Rd.,
Rewood City, CA 94062 (415) 299-8778
Breed Rescue: Gwen Arthur (713) 469-4214 (TX)

Staffordshire Bull Terrier Club, Inc.
Corres. Secretary: Catherine Swain, P.O. Box 5382, Montecito, CA 93150
Breeder Referral Contact: Marilyn Atwood, 24451 Dartmouth, Dearborn
Hights, MI 48125 (313) 277-3716
Breed Rescue: Tony George (718) 898-0298 (NY)

Welsh Terrier Club of America, Inc.
Corres.Secretary: Derry Coe, 9967 E. Ida Ave., Greenwood Village, CO
80111
Breeder Referral Contact: Same as above. (303) 721-3334
Breed Rescue: Ward & Carolyn Morris (404) 351-1330 (Ga.); Debi

Jamison (408) 725-0424 (CA)
West Highland White Terrier Club of America
Corres. Secretary: Ms. Anne Sander, 33101 44th Ave. NW, Stanwood, WA (360) 629 -2615 or 0-700-4WESTIE (AT&T access)
Breeder Referral Contact: Same as above
Breed Rescue: Anne Sanders (206) 629-2615 (WA)

AKC - Toy Group

Affenpinscher Club of America
Corres. Secretary: Sharon Strempski, 2 Tucktaway Ln., Danbury, CT 06810
Breeder Referral Contact: Ronald Carlson, 6114 Oliver Ave. S, Minneapolis, MN 55416 (612) 866-9606
Breed Rescue: Bernadine Hills (608) 455-1611 (WA)

American Brussels Griffon Association
Secretary: Terry J. Smith, P.O. Box 56, Grand Ledge, MI 48837
Breeder Referral Contact: Same as above. (517) 627-5916
Breed Rescue: Marjorie Simon (713) 783-8887 (TX)

American Cavalier King Charles Spaniel Club
Secretary: Martha Guimond, 1905 Upper Ridge Rd., Green Lane, PA 18054
Breeder Referral Contact: Yarrow Morgan, 5506 Trading Post Trail South, Afton, MN 55001 (612) 436-8326
Breed Rescue: None

Chihuahua Club of America, Inc.
Corres. Secretary: Lynnie Bunten, 5019 Village Trail, San Antonio, TX 78218
Breeder Referral Contact: Josephine DeMenna, 2 Maple St., Wilton, CT 06897 (203) 762-2314
Breed Rescue: Sharon Hermosillo (408) 251-6470 (CA)

American Chinese Crested Club, Inc.
Corres. Secretary: Kathleen Forth, Rt. 3 Box 157, Decatur, TX 76234
Breeder Referral Contact: Same as above. (817) 627-6772
Breed Rescue: Mary Mickelson 1-800-898-5266; (508) 874-5266 (MA)

English Toy Spaniel Club of America
Corres. Secretary: Ms. Susan Jackson, 18451 Sheffield Ln., Bristol, IN 46507-9455
Breeder Referral Contact: Ms. Christine Thaxton, 801 Greenwood Ave., Waukegan, IL 60087 (708) 662-1000
Breed Rescue: Mary Hoagland (609) 397-3148 (NJ)

Italian Greyhound Club of America, Inc.
Corres. Secretary: Lilian Barber, 35648 Menifee Rd., Murrieta, CA 92563
Breeder Referral Contact: Same as above. (909) 679-5084
Breed Rescue: Michelle Popka (219) 922-8147 (IN)

Japanese Chin Club of America
Secretary: Barbara Vallance, 1047 N. Stine Rd., Charlotte, MI 48813
Breeder Referral Contact: Mrs. Charla Cross, 3321 Huntleigh Dr., Raleigh, NC 27604 (919) 876-9336
Breed Rescue: Mimi Stauffer (918) 225-7374 (OK)

American Maltese Association, Inc.
Corres. Secretary: Pamela G. Rightmyer, 2211 S. Tioga Way, Las Vegas, NV 89117
Breeder Referral Contact: Same as above. (702) 256-0420
Breed Rescue: None

American Manchester Terrier Club
Secretary: Sandra Kipp, 5244 Rottinghaus Rd., Rt. 7, Waterloo, IA 50701
Breeder Referral Contact: Ms. Diana Haywood, 52 Hampton Rd., Pittstown, NJ 08867 (908) 996-7309
Breed Rescue: Patricia Hall (215) 957-0109 (PA)

Miniature Pinscher Club of America, Inc.
Secretary: Vivian A. Hogan, 26915 Clarksburg Rd., Damascus, MD 20872
Breeder Referral Contact: Betty Cottle, 332 McArthur Cir., Coca, FL 32927 (407) 632-6547
Breed Rescue: Joyce K. Somero (810) 656-4132 (MI)

Papillon Club of America, Inc.
Corres. Secretary: Mrs. Janice Dougherty, 551 Birch Hill Rd., Shoemakersville, PA 19555
Breeder Referral Contact: Same as above. (215) 926-5581

Breed Rescue: Diane Fuchs (904) 875-1422 (FL)
Pekingese Club of America, Inc.
Secretary: Mrs. Leonie Marie Schultz, Rt. #1, box 321, Bergton, VA 22811
Breeder Referral Contact: Mrs. Judith Pomato, 535 Devils, Ln., Ballston
Spa, NY 12020 (518) 885-6864
Breed Rescue: Dr. Claudia Covo (212) 362-3229 (NY)

American Pomeranian Club, Inc.
Corres. Secretary: Tim Goddard, Rt #2, Box 540, Opelosas, LA 70570-
9635
Breeder Referral Contact: Jane Lehtinen, 1325 9th St. S, Virginia, MN
55792 (218) 741-2117
Breed Rescue: Linda Brogoitti (602) 979-5336 (AZ)

Poodle Club of America, Inc.
Corres. Secretary: Mr. Charles Thomasson, 503 Martineau Dr., Chester,
VA 23831-5753
Breeder Referral Contact: Same as above. (804) 530-1605
Breed Rescue: Helen Taylor (713) 668-1021 (TX)

Pug Dog Club of America, Inc.
Secretary: Mr. James P. Cavalalro, 1820 Shadowlawn St., Jacksonville,
FL 32205
Breeder Referral Contact: Mary Ann Hall, 15988 Kettington Road,
Chesterfield, MO 63017-7350 (314) 207-1508;
E-mail: n2pug@worldnet.att.net
Breed Rescue: Ray & Pat Kolesar (715) 424-7847 (WI)

American Shi Tzu Club, Inc.
Corres. Secretary: Bonnie Prato, 5252 Shafter Ave., Oakland, CA 94618
Breeder Referral Contact: Andy Warner, 2 Big Oak Rd., Dillsburg, PA
17019 (717) 432-4351
Breed Rescue: Phyllis Celmer (619) 942-0874 (CA)

Silky Terrier Club of America, Inc.
Secretary: Ms. Louise Rosewell, 2783 S. Saulsbury St., Denver, CO 80227
Breeder Referral Contact: Same as above. (303) 988-4361
Breed Rescue: Dr. Braden Wolf (206) 756-5457 (WA)

Yorkshire Terrier Club of America, Inc.
Secretary: Mrs. Shirley A. Patterson, 2 Chestnut Ct., Star Rt., Pottstown, PA 19464
Breeder Referral Contact: Same as above. (610) 469-6781
Breed Rescue: None

AKC - Non-Sporting Group

American Eskimo Dog Club of America
Corres. Secretary: Barbara Beynon, 473 University Dr., Corpus Christi, TX 78414
Breeder Referral Contact: Carolyn Jester, Rt. #3 Box 211B, Stroud, OK 74079 (918) 968-3358
Breed Rescue: Sara Anderson (708) 851-8104 (IL)

Bichon Frise Club of America, Inc.
Corres. Secretary: Mrs. Bernice D. Richardson, 186 Ash Street N, Twin Falls, ID 83301
Breeder Referral Contact: Same as above. (208) 734-6262
Breed Rescue: Laura Fox-Meachen (414) 878-4446 (WI)

Boston Terrier Club of America
Corres. Secretary: Marian Sheehan, 8537 E. San Burno Dr., Scottsdale, AZ 85258
Breeder Referral Contact: Patricia Stone, 14792 Ronda Dr., San Jose, CA 95124 (408) 371-7452
Breed Rescue: Linda Trader 1-800-578-5088

Bulldog Club of America
Corres. Secretary: Toni Stevens, P.O. Box 248, Nobleton, FL 34661
Breeder Referral Contact: Susan Rodenski, 480 Bully Hill Dr., King George, VA 22485 (703) 775-3015
Breed Rescue: James & Diane Young (210) 340-0055 (TX)

Chinese Shar-Pei Club of America, Inc.
Secretary: Judy Dorough, 9806 Mission Blvd., Riverside, CA 92509
Breeder Referral Contact: Jocelyn Barker, P.O. Box 113809, Anchorage, AK 99511 (907) 345- 6504
Breed Rescue: Eastern Region: Charlene Rogers (203) 747-6397 (CT); Central Region: Bonnie Berney (918) 224-0820 (OK); Western Region: Dianne Gill (801) 798-3786 (UT); Dominion

Chinese Shar-Pei Club: Laura Prudom (757) 473-3587
Chow Chow Club, Inc.
Corres. Secretary: Irene Cartabio, 3580 Plover Pl., Seaford, NY 11783
Breeder Referral Contact: David Neilsen, RT #5 Box 563, Winnsboro, SC
29180 (803) 635-7047
Breed Rescue: Vicky Rodenberg (608) 756-2008 (WI)

Dalmation Club of America, Inc.
Corres. Secretary: Mrs. Sharon Boyd, 1303 James St., Rosenberg, TX
77471
Breeder Referral Contact: Mrs. Gerri Lightholder, 6109 W. 147th St., Oak
Forest, IL 60452 (708) 687-5447
Breed Rescue: Chris Jackson (410) 356-7252 (MD)

Finnish Spitz Club of America
Secretary: Peggy Urton, 8216 N. 50th Ave., Glendale, AZ 85302
Breeder Referral Contact: Sheila Goodwin, 5505 Glenlivet Pl.,
Greenville, TX 75402 (903) 455-7186
Breed Rescue: None

French Bulldog Club of America
Corres. Secretary: Diana H. Young, 5451 Vance Jackson Rd., San
Antonio, TX 78230
Breeder Referral Contact: Mr. Harry Dunn, Jr., 3638 Mayfair Dr.,
Tuscaloosa, AL 35404-5408 (205) 553-3817
Breed Rescue: Brenda Buckles (913) 383 1377

Keeshond Club of America, Inc.
Corres. Secretary: Tawn Sinclair, 11782 Pacific Coast Hwy., Malibu, CA
90265
Breeder Referral Contact: Pat Yagecic, 4726 B. Grant Ave., Philadelphia,
PA 19114 (215) 637-7731
Breed Rescue: Carole Henry (919) 742-7479 (NC)

American Lhasa Apso Club, Inc.
Corres. Secretary: Amy Andrews, 18105 Kirkshire, Beverly Hills, MI
48025
Breeder Referral Contact: None
Breed Rescue: Mary Schroeder (303) 973-3600 (CO)

Poodle Club of America, Inc.
Corres. Secretary: Mr. Charles Thomasson, 503 Martineau Dr., Chester,
VA 23831-5753
Breeder Referral Contact: None
Breed Rescue: Helen Taylor (713) 668-1021 (TX)

Schipperke Club of America, Inc.
Corres. Secretary: Dawn Hribar, 70480 Morency, Romeo MI 48065
Breeder Referral Contact: Margi Brinkley, 3245 8th St. S, Lebanon, OR
97355 (541) 259-3826
Breed Rescue: Shirley Smith (716) 985-4137 (NY)

National Shiba Club of America
Corres. Secretary: Kim Carlson, 526 Orchid Ct., Benicia, CA 94510
Breeder Referral Contact: Jacey Holden, 3991 W. Peltier Rd., Lodi, CA
95242 (209) 369-3473
Breed Rescue: None

Tibetan Spaniel Club of America
Corres. Secretary: Valerie Robinson, 103 Old Colony Dr., Mashpee, MA
02649
Breeder Referral Contact: Kay Dickeson, P.O. Box 427, Frisco, CO
80443 (970) 668-3364
Breed Rescue: Phyllis B. Kohler (540) 659-3265 (VA); Mallory Driskill
(804) 525-7710 (VA)

Tibetan Terrier Club of America
Secretary: Sharon Harrison, P.O. Box 528, Pleasanton, TX 78064
Breeder Referral Contact: Mrs. Trudy Erceg, 356 Laurel Park Pl.,
Hendersonville, NC 28791   (704) 692-5007
Breed Rescue: Ken Edmonds (404) 373-4605 (GA)

AKC - Herding Group

Australian Cattle Dog Club of America
Secretary: Gale J. Frost, 140 Cedar Cove Tr. #20, Lake St. Louis, MO
63367
Breeder Referral Contact: Nina Schroeder, 91 Sun Valley Rd., Tularosa,
NM 88352 (505) 585- 2186
Breed Rescue: Amy Berry (619) 366-3593 (CA)

United States Australian Shepherd Association
Secretary: Patricia Loomis, 7920 Peters Rd., Jacksonville, AR 72076
Breeder Referral Contact: None
Breed Rescue: None

Bearded Collie Club of America, Inc.
Corres. Secretary: Kathy Finley, 3232 E. Helena Dr., Phoenix, AZ 85032
Breeder Referral Contact: Same as above. (602) 992-1809
Breed Rescue: Paul Glatzer (516) 724-0871 (NY)

American Belgian Malinois Club
Corres. Secretary: Susan Morse, 7 Sunset West Circle, Ithaca, NY 14850
Breeder Referral Contact: Sharon Burke, 11605 Highview Ave.,
Wheaton, MD 20902 (301) 946-0195
Breed Rescue: Allyson Olson (801) 326-4243

Belgian Sheepdog Club of America, Inc.
Corres. Secretary: Marilyn Russell, RFD 2, Bos 2480, Bangor, ME 04401
Breeder Referral Contact: Same as above. (207) 848-5613
Breed Rescue: Sharon Roundy (708) 343-3358 (IL); Robin Barfoot (517)
627-2549 (MI)

American Belgian Tervuren Club, Inc.
Corres. Secretary: Karen Johnson, P.O. Box 174, Walled Lake, MI 48390
Breeder Referral Contact: Same as above. (810) 685-3648
Breed Rescue: Cindy Simonsen (414) 642- 2286 (WI)

The Border Collie Society of America
Corres. Secretary: Nancy Gagliardi Little, 8860 James Court, Chicago
City, MN 55013
Breeder Referral Contact: None
Breed Rescue: Jo Ellen Wolf (706) 863-0951 (GA)

American Bouvier des Flandres Club, Inc.
Corres. Secretary: Dorothy Kent, 10520 West 102nd Place, Westminster,
CO 80021-3717
Breeder Referral Contact: Same as above. (303) 466-1242
Breed Rescue: Dianne Sutherland (713) 852-8521 (Texas)

Briard Club of America, Inc.
Corres. Secretary: Sue Wahr, 1 Seneca Cir., Andover, MA 01810
Breeder Referral Contact: Sharon Wise, 31 High St., Winthrop, ME
04364-1322 (207) 377-8689
Breed Rescue: Merry Jean Millner (910) 869-5490 or (910) 841-7392 (NC)

Collie Club of America, Inc.
Corres. Secretary: Carmen Leonard, 1119 South Fleming Rd.,
Woodstock, IL 60098
Breeder Referral Contact: Same as above. (815) 337-0323;
E-mail SECCCA@aol.com
Breed Rescue: Linda Knouse (215) 659-3331 (PA)

German Sheperd Dog Club of America, Inc.
Corres. Secretary: Blanche Beisswenger, 17 West Ivy Lane, Englewood,
NJ 07631
Breeder Referral Contact: Same as above. (201) 568-5806
Breed Rescue: Linda Kury (408) 247-1272 (CA)

Old English Sheepdog Club of America, Inc.
Corres. Secretary: Kathryn Bunnell, 14219 E. 79th St. S., Derby, KS
67037
Breeder Referral Contact: Ms. Joan Long, 5704 Greenwood, Shawnee,
KS 66216 (913) 631-614
Breed Rescue: Laurie McCain (410) 923-6181 (MD)

Puli Club of America, Inc.
Secretary: Mrs. Patricia Giancaterino, 134 Mitchell Ave., Runnemede, NJ
08078; E-mail: pulidog@aol.com
Breeder Referral Contact: Same as above. (609) 939-3096
Breed Rescue: Betty O'Donnell (207) 283-3528 (ME)

American Shetland Sheepdog Association
Corres. Secretary:Mr. George Page, 1100 Cataway Pl., Bryans Road, MD
20616
Breeder Referral Contact: Mrs. Joyce Kern 1879 cole Rd., Aromas, CA
95004 (408) 726-1660
Breed Rescue: Dorothy Christiansen (815) 485-3726 (IL)

Cardigan Welsh Corgi Club of America
Corres. Secretary: Ginny Conway, 14511 Trophey Club Dr., Houston, TX 77095-3420
Breeder Referral Contact: Tricia Olson, 5512 La Plata Cir., Boulder, CO 80301 (303) 530-7107
Breed Rescue: H. Pamela Allen (703) 836-1963 (VA)

Pembroke Welsh Corgi Club of America, Inc.
Corres. Secretary: Joan Gibson Reid, 9589 Sheldon Rd., Elk Grove, CA 95624
Breeder Referral Contact: Same as above. (916) 689-1661
Breed Rescue: Betty Hall (907) 376-0529 (home); (907) 273-7276 (work); (AK)

Non-AKC/Rare Breed Clubs

American Dog Breeders Assoc. (Pit Bull Terrier) - 180 S. Hwy 89 N, Salt Lake City, UT 84054

Anatolian Shepherd Dog Club of America - Quinn S. Harned, P.O. Box 1271, Alpine, CA 91903   (619) 445-3334

Appenzeller Mountain Dog Club of America - Bill Coleman, Box 279A1 RD 1, Pedricktown, NJ 08067 (609) 299-7197

Argentino Dogo Club of America, Inc. - 2014 Albany St., Lafayette, IN 47904

American Azawakh Assoc. - Debra Rookard, P.O. Box 312, Thornburg, VA 22656-0312

Basque Shepherd Club of America - RD 1 Box 101E Long, Eddy, NY 12760-9637

North American Beauceron Club - Susan Bulanda, 106 Halteman Rd., Pottstown, PA 19464 (215) 323-6725

Bleu de Gascogne Club or America - E.S. Traverse, RT 1 Box 28, Castleton, VT 05735 (802) 468-5484

Bolognese Club of America - Box 1461, Montrose, CO 81402
Canaan Dog Club of America - Lorraine Stephens, Box 555, Newcastle,

OK 73065-0555

United States Cane Corse Club & Registry - Sandra Freeman, 5107 Darkmoor, Imperial, MO 63052 (314) 464-3275

Caucasian Ovtcharka Club of America - P.O. Box 745, Painesville, OH 44077

Cesky Terrier Club of America - Lori Moody, P.O. Box 1318, Goldsboro, NC 27534

Chinook Owners Assoc. - Grace Anderson, PO Box 3282, Jackson, WY 83001 (307) 733-3182

The Coton de Tulear Club of America - P.O. Box 7152, Van Nuys, CA 91409-7152 (818) 988-8978

Dogo Argentino Club of America - Jose Ricardo Vidal, Rt 2 Box 11, Goodland, IN 47948

Entlebucher Club of America - RD 2 Box 899 RT 206, Chester, NJ 07930 (201) 584-1229

Fila Brasileiro Club of America - 244 Flat Rock Church Rd., Zebulon, GA 30295 (706) 567-8085

American German Pinscher Breeders Assoc. - Rhonda Parks, 701 Calvin Ave., Portage, PA 15946 (814) 736-9699

Original Havanese Club - Joseph Sleziak, 40667 Newport Dr., Plymouth, MI 48170-4742

Italian Spinone Club - Mr. Jim Channon, PO Box 307, Warsaw, VA 22572 (804) 333-0309

Jack Russell Terrier Club of America - P.O. Box 4527, Lutherville, MD 21094-4527 (410) 561-3655 (Initial contact with Russell Rescue is to be made at the above address also.)

JinDo - Barbara Abrams, 16815 Germantown Rd., Germantown, MD 20874 (301) 972-1423

National Kai Ken Club - PO Box 217, Maximo, OH 44650

Karelian Bear Dog - Arlene Sherrod, 1550 Bitterroot Dr., Marion, MT 59925 (406) 854-2240

Working Kelpies, Inc. - Cindy Vondette, RT 3 Box 243, Willard, MO 65781

Lapphund Club of America - Linda Marden, 1870 Locke-Cuba Rd., Millington, TN 38053 (901)876-3205

Leonberger Club of America - Marlene Stuteville, PO Box 97, Georgetown, CT 06829-0097

Little Lion Dog Club of America - Sandra Lunka, 2771 Graylock Dr., Willoughby Hills, OH44094 (216) 951-5288

National Association of Louisiana Catahoulas - PO Box 1041, Denham Springs, LA 70727

Magyar Agar Club of America - Lance House, 2280 Grass Valley Hwy #230, Auburn CA 95603

Norwegian Buhund Club of America - Mrs. Jan Christoferson Barringer, RR1 Box 8A, Bethalto, IL 62010-9801 (618) 466-3777

Norwegian Lundehund Club of America, Inc. - Harvey Sanderson, 33 Amsterdam Rd., Milford, NJ 08848 (908) 995-7422

Nova Scotia Duck Tolling Retriever Club - Gretchen Botner, 951 Moon Ct., Marco Island, FL 33937

National American Pit Bull Terrier Assoc. - Patti Murley, Rt 2 Box 1157, Denton, TX 76201 (817) 387-2107

Polish Owczarek Nizinny Club - Kaz and Betty Augustowski, 1115 Delmont Rd., Severn, MD 21144 (410) 551-6750

Polish Tatra Sheepdog Club of America - Carol Wood, N 11724 Forker Rd., Spokane, WA 99207

Pyrenean Shepherd Club of America - Mrs. Jean Cave-Pero, 4501 Old Pond Dr., Plano, TX 75024-4708

American Sloughi Association - Vicki Barter, PO Box 308, North Liberty, IA 52317-0308

Slovak Tchouvatch Dog Club of America - Joseph and Maya Schon, 49 Old Middletown Rd., Nanuet, NY 10954 (914) 623-8185

Spanish Mastiff Club of America - 1045 RT 18, New Brunswick, NJ 08816

Spinone Italiano - PO Box 284, Carmel, IN 48032

Swedish Vallhund Enthusiasts of America - Mr. and Mrs. John B. Thell, RR1 Box 102 Waterman Hill Rd., Greene, RI 02827 (401) 397-5003

Telomian Dog Club of American - Audrey Palumbo, 28765 White Rd., Perrysburg, OH 43551

Treeing Walker Breeders and Fanciers Association - Connie Wade, PO Box 399, Guy TX 77444 (409) 793-4133

Appendix B: Sources for Adult Purebread Dogs Dog Tracks and National Greyhound Placement Organizations

Dog Tracks:An increasing number of dog tracks and racing kennels are running and financially supporting their own placement kennels. Some of these kennels are on-site, some are nearby. Other times, a dog track will work directly with a local placement organization, giving the organization funding, office space, and kennels at the track. If you live near a track that is not listed in this appendix, call and ask if the track runs a placement service. If not, the track operators should be able to provide you with the names and numbers of placement agencies with which they work.

Greyhound Placement Organizations: The number of Greyhound rescues has mushroomed in the past five years to well over a 100 groups operating in the United States. Some of the groups are in for the "long haul," while many others burn out quickly. The numbers listed in this appendix are for the national networks that keep tabs on who is doing what in all parts of the country. Not all groups are affiliated with these national organizations. To find a local group that is not listed with these national networks, call your local shelter for more information or ask a local veterinarian. Most rescues give their information to these two sources.

Dog Tracks
Alabama
Birmingham Race Course, 1000 John Rogers Drive, Birmingham, AL 35210; McGregor Greyhound Welfare Center, Greyhound Pets of America, 1-800-366-1472 or (205) 833-6654

VictoryLand, P.O. Box 128, Shorter, AL 36075-0128; Adopt-A-Greyhound, Mary Mansour, (334) 409-0622.

Arizona
Arizona Adopt-A-Greyhound, Phoenix Greyhound Park, 3801 East Washington St., Phoenix, AZ 85034-1796. (602) 971-6935. (Program shared by two tracks)

Colorado
Recycled Racers, Mile High Kennel Club, 6200 Dahlia St., Commerce City, CO 80022-3197; (303)-288-1591. (Program shared by three tracks)

Connecticut
Plainfield Pets, Plainfield Greyhound Park, P.O. Box 205, Plainfield, CT 06374-0205; (860) 564-5640.

Florida
Daytona Beach Kennel Club, Greyhound Pets of America, P.O. Box 11470, Daytona Beach, FL 32120-1470, Sandy Snyman, (904) 239-3647.

Jacksonville Greyhound Racing, Greyhounds as Pets of Northeast Florida, Inc., PO Box 5424, Jacksonville, FL 32245-4249 1-904-389-2934 (24-hour answering service)

Hollywood Greyhound Track, Holly Dogs, 1600 S. Dixie Hwy., Hollywood, FL 30020, (954) 925-7758.

Melbourne Greyhound Park, 110 N. Wickham Rd., Melbourne, FL 32935, Greyhound Pets of America, (407) 259-9800

Palm Beach Kennel Club, 1111 North Congress Ave., West Palm Beach, FL 33409, Greyhound Pets of America, 1-800-366-1472. (An off-site facility)

Pensacola Greyhound Track Adoption Program, P.O. Box 12824, Pensacola, FL 32575-2824, Kim Kenney or Margaret Sheilds, (904) 455-8595

Sanford-Orlando Kennel Club, SOKC Greyhound Adoption, P.O. Box 520280, Longwood, FL 32752, (407) 382-7529.

Sarasota Kennel Club, Inc., REGAP, 5400 Bradenton Rd., Sarasota, FL 34234-2999, (914) 379-FAST.

Seminole Greyhound Park, Greyhound Pets of America, Lisa Nolet, P.O. Box 151021, Altamonte Springs, FL 32715, (407) 332-4754.

St. Petersburg Kennel Club, Greyhound Pets of America, Derby Lane, 10490 Gandy Blvd., St. Petersburg, FL 33702-2395, (813) 576-4300.

Iowa
Bluffs Run, Bluffs Run Casino Adopt-A-Greyhound Program, Attn: Donna Lovely, P.O. Box 396, Pacific Junction, Iowa 51561 (712) 622-8334.

Dubuque Greyhound Park, Dubuque Greyhound Park Adoption Program, P.O. Box 3190, Dubuque, IA 52004-3190, (319) 582-3647.

Kansas
The Woodlands, Pups Without Partners, P.O. Box 12036, Kansas City, KS 66112 (913) 299-9797.

Wichita Greyhound Park, Wichita Greyhound Park Adoption Center, P.O. Box 277, Valley Center, KS 67147-0277, (316) 755-4000.

New Hampshire
Hinsdale Greyhound Park, REGAP, Norman DuPont, P.O. Box 27, Hinsdale, NH 03451-0027; 1-800-NH-TRACK.

Lake Region Greyhound Track, P.O. Box 280, Belmont, NH 03220-0280, Greyhound Pets of America, 1-800-366-1472. (Seasonal track: May - Sept.)

Seabrook Greyhound Park, REGAP, P.O. Box 219, Seabrook, NH 03874-0219, Chris Marshall, (603) 474-3065 ext 207.

Rhode Island
Lincoln Greyhound Park, Lincoln Greyhound Adoption, 1600 Louisquisset Pike, Lincoln, RI 02865-4506, Norm Deragon or Steve Machowski, (401) 723-3200.

Texas
Corpus Christi Greyhound Track, Corpus Christi Greyhound Adoption Program, P.O. Box 9087, Corpus Christi, Texas 78469 (512) 289-9333.

West Virginia
Tri-State Greyhound Park, Tri-State Greyhound Park Adoption Program, 1 Greyhound Drive, Cross Lanes, WV 25356-7118, 1-800-224-9683

Wheeling Downs Greyhound Park, Greyhound Pets of America, S. Penn and Stone St., Wheeling, WV 26003, Lou Batdorf, (304) 232-5050 ext. 217.

Wisconsin
Geneva Lakes Greyhound Track, Geneva Lakes Greyhound Track Adoption Program, P.O. Box 650, Delavan, WI 53115, Betty Schmidt, (414) 728-8000.

St. Croix Meadows Greyhound Racing Park, St. Croix Meadow Adoption Center, P.O. Box 750, Hudson, WI 54016, (715) 386-6800.

National Greyhound Placement Organizations Greyhound Pets of America: 5 Carleton Avenue, Randolph, MA 02368 1-800-366-1472

Greyhound Friends, Inc.: 167 Saddle Hill Road, Hopkinton, MA 01748 (508) 435-5969

Make Peace With Animals: Cynthia Branigan, (215) 862-0605 (PA)

REGAP (Retired Greyhounds As Pets): P.O. Box 41307, St. Petersburg, FL 33743   (813) 347-2206

Appendix C:
Sources for Adult Mixed-Breed Dogs
Rescue Organizations

To find your local pound, look under the blue government pages in your phone book under the listing, "Animal Control." To find the non-profit, private shelters in your area, look in the Yellow Pages under "Humane Organizations."

The following is a list of national humane organizations.

The American Humane Association - 63 Inverness Drive East, Englewood, CO 80112 (303) 792-9900

American Humane Education Society - 350 S. Huntington Avenue, Boston, MA 02130 (617) 522-7400

American Society for the Prevention of Cruelty to Animals - 441 E. 92nd Street, New York, NY 10128 (212) 876-7700

The Doris Day Animal League - 900 2nd Street NE, Suite 303, Washington, DC 20002 (202) 842-3325

Friends of Animals, Inc. - P.O. Box 1244, Norwalk, CT 06856 (203) 866-5223

The Humane Society of the United States - 2100 L Street NW, Washington, DC 20037 (202) 452-1100

National Humane Education Society - 521A East Market Street, Leesburg, VA 22075 (703) 777-8319

Pets Are Wonderful Council (P.A.W.) - 500 N. Michigan Avenue, Suite 200, Chicago, IL 60611 (312) 836-7145

Appendix D
Sixteen Ways You Can
Help Breed Rescue

Whether or Not You Adopt a Dog
1. Make a donation.
2. Sign on as a foster home.
3. Offer to provide transportation to and from shelters, vets, and foster homes.
4. Photocopy materials for adoption and information packets.
5. Provide grooming services.
6. Are you an attorney? Legal services are always at a premium . . .
7. Share your obedience training expertise and make a rescue dog more placeable.
8. Make an in-kind donation (Crates, collars, leashes, food, etc.).
9. Share your fundraising expertise with breed rescue.
10. Help with rescue education by distributing flyers, breed information, posters, etc.
11. Be a rescue ambassador! Take your rescued dog wherever you go. ("I'm a rescued dog" bandanas and collars are pretty attention-grabbing.) Be sure to carry business cards with the phone number of the breed rescue to hand out and be well-educated! You'll want to be sure you're giving out the right information.
12. Assist with the breed rescue newsletter; writers, graphic artists, and printers are always welcome!
13. Offer to mail out applications or interview applicants over the telephone.
14. Perform home screenings and one-month checkups.
15. Serve as a shelter "scout" and alert rescue when there is a breed member in the shelter.
16. Assist with shelter relations. Present a very professional, caring image in order to encourage shelters to work with your group (as opposed to against your group).

Appendix E
Six Ways You Can Help Your Local Shelter
Whether or Not You Adopt A Dog

1. Donate! A little money can go a long way. (Of course, a lot of money goes even farther . . .)
2. Offer your time. Volunteers are always needed.
3. Open your home. Consider becoming a foster parent to a dog in need.
4. Share your expertise. Do you specialize in a field that could help your shelter? Whether you are an artist, an ad exec, a lawyer or perhaps a carpenter, plumber or just a good "fixer," your skills could be put to very good use - if you are willing!
5. Fundraising. Maybe you don't have a whole lot of money to give, but you're good at getting other people or corporations to assist good causes! Your shelter can use your help!
6. Training & Education. Part of the battle is teaching the public the importance of spay/neuters, what being a GOOD pet owner is all about, and how to train a dog to be a good companion. If you enjoy public speaking or have special skills and can offer training classes to shelter workers and/or new adoptive parents, call your shelter!